What People Are Saying...

"In facing loss of loved ones, suicide, loneliness, abandonment, we find ourselves murmering 'Oh that's why!' It is then we 'get it.' God is the God of perfect timing. Anita tells her amazing story of her relationship with her mother from the perspective of wisdom learned when she couldn't praise Him for what He allowed but let the pain drive her to an all sufficient Christ! A must read."

—JILL BRISCOE, AUTHOR AND INSPIRE WOMEN'S SPIRITUAL MOM

"Anita Carman's story is an incredible journey of God's grace and ultimately His placement of her as a woman of influence. God is using Anita and Inspire Women in big ways, but every step of the path has not been easy. Impact is forged in the furnace of perseverance. We live step by step taking our hurts, dreams and joys to Jesus allowing Him to make sense of them. A Daughter's Destiny is a journey of steps of grace leading to a life of impact."

—KELLY MATTE, WIFE OF GREGG MATTE, SENIOR PASTOR OF HOUSTON'S FIRST BAPTIST CHURCH

"I welcomed a novelized approach to teachings from a story that is compelling, intriguing, and connects to the base instincts of curiosity and the longing for answers that makes us want to buy a book and read it. And now I know my mother's story and my story are inextricably connected."

—DEBORAH CLIFTON, CEO OF TARRENPOINT

"I was pulled in from the first sentence. This story gave me much to ponder about my own life."

—GEORGIANA NICHOLS, FORMER PRESIDENT OF CENTERPOINT ENERGY

"Anita's writing depicts her love for God and her enthusiasm for sharing her life for God's glory. If you have ever longed to add meaning and significance to your purpose as a woman of God, this book will encourage you to allow God to lead you on your journey."

—RUBY AUGUST, FIRST LADY OF THE CHURCH AT BETHEL'S FAMILY

A DAUGHTER'S
DESTINY

*Finding Redemption
in the Midst of Broken Dreams*

ANITA CARMAN

Library of Congress Control Number: 2016916812

Carman, Anita
A Daughter's Destiny/Anita Carman
ISBN 978-0-9772905-6-7
Copyright © 2016 by Dreams Won't Die, LLC

Printed in the United States of America

SAN 257-1439
Published by Inspire Women
1415 S. Voss, # 110-516
Houston, TX 77057

Inspire Women does not accept unsolicited manuscripts.

For additional copies of
A Daughter's Destiny
or to contact Anita Carman for a speaking engagement
please visit www.inspirewomen.org or call 713-521-0690.

Written
in memory of my mother
who gave me life and
shaped my story.
Mother, I will always love you!

A Daughter's Destiny

Introduction

As women, we are all daughters forever. Our stories are intertwined with our mothers' stories. Our lives become revisions and re-visitations of their lives. Many of us are daughters of trauma, daughters of failed hopes, daughters who have borne the burden of running the paths that our mothers couldn't. How do we cope with this complex legacy?

Many times, we simply don't. We don't know how to, or we think that time and forgetfulness alone will heal us. So many women, myself included, run towards the compelling distractions of achievement or devotion to others. I spent my young adulthood running from my mother's tragedy at the same time that I subconsciously tried to resolve it. I finished college in two years, got my MBA, and dived into a life of corporate consulting. I threw myself in and out of relationships that failed miserably—never realizing that I was a half-empty vessel, waiting in futility for romantic love to fill the ache in my heart and the gap in my soul.

Then I grew older and stronger. I found my spiritual compass, my purpose in life, and a mission grounded in God's love for His daughters. I began to read the Bible as love letters from God. I went to seminary, submerged myself in discovering the family history of my Heavenly Father, and realized that I had another, more powerful legacy to uphold.

In time, I understood that as a child of God, I was the daughter of a King with a blessed place in God's family tree. I was created for more than my mother's dreams because God did not create me for my mother but for Himself. From this place of divine purpose I found the security to trace the details of my mother's story to find closure for the dangling threads of my life. I wanted to understand what it meant to be a woman who had never been given any help to deal with her losses and who had sacrificed everything she possessed for me, including even her life. I needed to understand how a woman's mind could have become so confused, so desperate, that she killed herself as a misguided act of love and protection.

In unraveling the details of my mother's lost dreams, I salute my mother as a woman who fought battles and sometimes lost. We are fellow women who have been given life and potential as well as the blessed freedom to choose what we want to do with these things.

This book is about my mother's dreams and disappointments—about the unexpected threads that connected her to me and to the lives of thousands of women today. It is both her tragedy and her song of hope.

This is my mother's story. But in understanding it, I release her and find my own. I emerge from the ashes of her lost dreams to step into my place as daughter of God The King—empowered by my Heavenly Father to move from victim to victor, from helplessness to being a royal ambassador of God's hope, goodness, and mercy to the world.

A Daughter's Destiny: Finding Redemption in the Midst of Broken Dreams will open doors to discussions about your relationships with significant people in your formative years. It will open your eyes to see God's presence in the broken scripts of unfinished stories and the vision of what could be when you allow your Heavenly Father to finish your story in His redemptive way.

CHAPTER 1

Born a Daughter

I was seventeen the night it happened.

It happened in Hong Kong, on an unsuspecting day in 1974, six months before I would leave for America to attend Mississippi University for Women on a long sought-after scholarship. It happened just before dawn, in the dim hours when the world still wears the blanket of night. In the bedroom I shared with my older sister, I woke up suddenly, hearing a wailing cry. My father was shouting my sister's name. I shook her awake and we timidly groped our way through our house, our hearts pounding in the presence of the unknown. In the living room I stood frozen as my sister made her way into the kitchen. I heard my father's ragged voice saying, "Quick! Get a knife! Cut her down!" as he held up her body to keep the rope from choking her any further. My mother had hung herself from the rafters.

I stood in our living room, feeling like the ground beneath my feet was crumbling. America had been my mother's dream. America had been all she had ever hoped for, the sole devotion of her scarred and broken life. And we were almost there. My sister and I had been accepted into college already, and we felt certain that we'd be able to help our parents make the crossing. After all those years of courageous dreaming and painful sacrifices, why had she given up now?

With my father holding her ankles, my sister cut down her body. Blood and cords and limbs, all of us sobbing in this house, now wrapped in tragedy. Death covered me in all its heaviness and permanence. I felt helplessly trapped in the midst of this nightmare, asking myself questions that would consume me, night after night, for decades to come.

Six months after her death, I left the city where I was born, not realizing I had stepped into a plan my mother put in motion the day I was born. I found refuge on a university campus with professors who invested in my potential. Even while the ashes were still smoldering from the dreams my mother burned to the ground by her fatal act, I was my mother's success story. My new beginning was the result of her years of planning and training me to succeed in the world of academia. But why, I asked, did she have to die for me to live?

My mother was born in a village as far from America as you can imagine. The village in the town of HeXien, AnHui province China was damp and sleepy, a patchwork of sweet potato and wheat fields that were often ruined by the powerful floodwaters from the thundering Yangtze River at least once a year. Before sunrise, small lights appeared in windows as the poor farmers prepared for a full day bending over sprouted leaves and woven baskets. They took a break at midday and ate lunch squatted on the ground, standing up occasionally to stretch their backs. Then they went back to work with their minds blank and their tired bodies ready to toil again. At night, the women made tea in their huts and would pour steaming cups for their men and children. They counted their seeds, counted their money, and found that it was never enough.

On the evening of my mother's birth, it was late winter and the sky was a drained, colorless grey. The year was 1925 and China was divided by old struggles and new ideas. There was trouble brewing near the village, a squabble between competing militias. A group of taciturn men sat outside their houses in the dusk and listened to horses galloping in the distance. Cries of pain floated down the street, coming from the dilapidated house where my family lived, as my mother was being born.

"Another mouth to feed," said one man absentmindedly.

"Earth finds use for whatever Heaven makes," another said.

The men chuckled mirthlessly. What would Earth do with another girl? There were already too many children in the village.

In the little house, the new baby wailed. The women of the family cleaned up the mess, scrubbing blood and sweat from the floor. My grandmother cradled the fat-cheeked, red-faced infant, the first child of the new generation. Her husband tickled the baby's chin without commenting and headed off to sleep, politely hiding his disappointment. He, like everyone, had hoped for a boy.

7

My grandmother stared at the baby girl's tiny hands. Would they be the hands of a peasant farmer or a real lady?

It would depend upon how pretty the girl turned out to be.

Years passed and the girl became beautiful—so beautiful that she attracted attention wherever she went. She was lively and imaginative, with an intellectual spark that surprised both of her parents. She took care of her siblings, born one after the other like clockwork until there were four additional mouths to feed. She supervised the cleaning and cooking, she saved scraps of fabric to make little dolls, and she amused her little sisters with stories of far-away places.

My exhausted grandmother grew to love my mother very much, but no one loved her more than my great grandfather, a well-regarded elder of the community. He and my mother took walks together at sunset, counting clouds and naming the hills in the distance. With the wisdom and good humor that allowed my great grandfather to peacefully settle neighborly disputes and family squabbles over inheritance, he cautioned my mother against burning her mouth on her morning porridge and teased her about falling into the outhouse pit at night. She followed his advice obediently. She understood, even at the age of seven, that my great grandfather was venerated among the people in the local community. But she didn't understand how special he had been until the day he died.

On that day, the house was silent but terribly busy, with the women running around with frozen faces to tidy up before the mourners came. The body was in the living room, and the children were not allowed to see it. No one bothered to explain the death to my mother, a little girl who had been my great grandfather's favorite.

"But how *exactly?*" my mother asked, the panic rising in her voice as she trailed my grandmother from room to room. "And it's *forever?*"

People began to gather at the family's house. The villagers were all poor, but their hands were full of gifts. They brought bowls of fresh eggs. They brought their fattest chickens. A few of them even brought pigs. Then the people started trickling in from far away, all bearing gifts that were, in reality, too much for each humble family to afford. The people wept and mourned the old man as the bright day turned to dusk, then darkened to black night.

My mother watched, small and forgotten, as the village honored her grandfather. There were eggs piled up everywhere; the chicken coop was full to bursting. Before she went to bed that night, she approached her mother, whose face was swollen and looked like a bruise. "Why did they bring us eggs and chickens?"

"When somebody loves you," her mother said sadly, "they give you whatever they have. These eggs and chickens are like the gifts for a king. Remember how much your grandfather was loved. Remember how much honor he brought to this family." Her mother's face crumpled again. "And now we're left with your father, who can't even hold down a job for two days!"

Soon after this, my mother's family moved to Shanghai. Without the respectable presence of their old patriarch, the family's name—as my grandmother predicted—had been swiftly dragged into the mud by the never-ending business failures of my mother's father.

First, he had worked for the railroad company, always getting in trouble with one supervisor or another, or sleeping too late, or forgetting to come in for special projects. He was fired again and again. Then he decided to change careers. He tried to learn traditional Chinese medicine, but could not master even the Six Excesses or the Eight Principles. He mixed up his diagnoses, telling patients first that they had too much internal wind, then changed to say they suffered from an excess of heat and dampness. He prescribed incorrect herbs. When he gave the schoolmaster a stomachache that lasted for three weeks, my grandmother was crushed by this humiliation, the latest example of her husband's incompetence. Why hadn't he gotten any of his father's abilities? She didn't ask this question, but she wore it on her face plainly. The look of shame she wore around the house was so pitiful that he decided his family needed nothing so much as a fresh start.

But in Shanghai life was even more difficult. Inflation was absolutely horrendous and life was unimaginably chaotic. Posted prices of rice rose three times a day. Hawkers of silver coins at every other street corner were barking incessantly at passersby about the ever changing exchange rates. On a daily basis, wages paid in yuan were converted to silver coins immediately to protect against devaluation. Silver coins were then converted back into yuan to buy food. As the government continued to print more and more money, there was a total collapse of the economy. My grandmother held back her feelings as my grandfather looked fruitlessly for a job. He found temporary things here and there—cleaning up after hours at a bank, delivering dry goods for a store —but he believed that this work was beneath him, which infuriated his supervisors and caused him to get fired, again and again. "I'm a doctor," he'd spit out at the end of another day, when his wife asked him about work. "They can take their delivery bicycle and they can shove it!"

My grandmother started sobbing whenever he started to talk like this, knowing that he'd lost another job. My mother, now nine years old, scurried away. She was doing well in school and didn't understand why her life couldn't just be normal. The way the other girls talked, it seemed like they never had to worry about where their next bowl of rice was coming from. She wanted to make friends with these girls, but didn't know how. It was like she didn't come with the right story, the right background, or the right mannerisms.

One night, my mother was lying on a pallet in the room she shared with her siblings, who were outside playing in the street. She was listening to her parents argue brutally, as they had been doing night after night.

Dusk fell. The blackness in the corners of the room seemed to be creeping towards her. She couldn't stand this life, this room that seemed to be choking her, the chicken-squawk voices of her parents arguing about money, money, money. My mother stood up suddenly and ran out the door of the house, ignoring her brothers' and sisters' attempts to grab her and ask her where she was going.

Where was she going? She didn't know. She vaguely thought of the aunt who lived close to them. She tried to recall the path. They had gone to visit her shortly after moving to Shanghai. She looked for markers—the yellow storefront, the apartment with the rusty door, the low-hanging clothesline. The streets were dirty and cramped, full of debris and rogue chickens. She turned down alleyways, passing people quickly and ignoring the men who said things to her. She arrived at a door that she thought was her aunt's. She knocked.

The door opened. "Oh, you!" said her aunt, a short woman with a round, skeptical face. "What are you doing here?"

My mother couldn't help but peer into the house. Though the space was ordinary, it was tidy and well decorated. She pictured her own disordered, ramshackle home and felt a pang of shame.

"Are you going to say something? You, little girl?"

"I—I wanted to—" My mother's voice trailed off. She didn't know what she was doing. "I just—things are tough at home—"

"Ah. You need money, is that why you've come?"

My mother looked at her aunt, whose eyes were full of thinly veiled contempt, and realized that she had indeed come for money. What else?

"What's wrong with your father, anyway?" the aunt asked.

She looked at her feet, trying to swallow her anger and humiliation.

"It's really such a shame that he can't hold down a job, and that his daughter has to come begging in the street like a common whore," the aunt said.

My young mother looked up, feeling like she'd been slapped. "I'm sorry for bothering you," she said. She turned and walked away, picking up her pace to leave this awful house behind as fast as possible.

"Wait!" called her aunt. "Wait, I'm sorry. I mean you no harm—it's just that lazy father of yours, he makes me sick.

Wait here." The aunt walked into the house, leaving the door wide open. My mother stared into the entryway, which had beautiful black-and-white drawings framed in sleek golden boxes. Pretty little plants sat on the windowsills, growing fat and content. Her aunt returned carrying a small sack of rice. "Take this to fill your belly."

"Thank you," my mother said quietly, steeling herself against the shame she felt. "Thank you very much."

Her aunt shut the door.

It was fully nighttime by this point, and my mother made her way back through shadowy streets, throwing rocks to scare the stray dogs nipping at her heels. When she arrived at her house, she opened the door to find her family sitting around the dinner table, sipping cups of thin broth. She held up the sack of rice.

Her mother ran to her, pulling her into the sooty kitchen with a look of puzzled, painful relief. "How did you get this?"

"I went to Auntie's house," my mother said.

Her mother clasped her close, stroking her hair in a rare display of affection. "My sweet girl," she said. "My sweet girl, who understands the pain of this world."

"It's okay," she said. "Auntie's not very nice."

"She's terrible," said her mother. "I'm sure she asked you to pay with your dignity for this food. Remember this: you know who your friends are when you have to beg for a bowl of rice."

From that night on, my mother gave up hoping that her father would get a job. She decided to quit school and work during the day to help her mother. She did this in secret for the first few months. When her mother began to understand what her oldest daughter had done, she hugged her tightly again but made no mention of her ever returning to school. They needed the money, and they needed the rice. Having her young daughter work was much better than having her beg— which she had done on a few humiliating evenings, when the family's pantry was completely empty and not a single neighbor would lend them any food.

In her first job, which lasted three years, my mother scrubbed the kitchen of a nearby cafe. It was good work, because she could eat the leftovers for dinner and sometimes even bring some home. One of the cooks had a nice-looking son who came in after school to help prepare dinner. They struck up a friendship. The boy was respectful and intelligent. He had a surprising sense of humor that made my mother feel at home, like someone finally understood that it was important not to take everything so seriously. She would ask him about what he had learned in school that day, and he would teach her little pieces of his lessons. "I'm going to go to the United States one day," he said.

"I wish I could do that," she said.

That night, my mother went home late, carrying her pittance of rice. She scrubbed her face at the washstand and imagined living in the United States as a wife to the nice-looking boy from the restaurant. She looked at herself for a rare, lingering moment, noticing the delicacy of her jaw line and the deep richness of her eyes. It wasn't so hard to imagine that this boy would think of her as beautiful. They could have sweet, hard-working children who would grow up in the perfect American school system and become rich and successful doctors. She would never have to worry about her husband being too lazy or shiftless to work. Every night he would come home and take her into his arms and tell her she was beautiful.

Barely turning twelve, she woke up the next morning with a sunburst of blood on her blankets. She carried the blankets outside, where her mother saw them, and cried silently.

When my mother went into work at the cafe later, she felt too sick and strange to talk with her friend normally. All she could think about was the way she was getting older, the way things were happening to her that she hated and couldn't control, and how unfair it was that she'd been born a girl.

My mother's next job was in a hotel, a seedy place that housed second-tier businessmen traveling through Shanghai. She worked as a maid. It was tough on her hands, and the job was lonely—as a maid, she was supposed to be invisible—but she didn't mind the solitude. It gave her time to think about saving money, and what she would do when she had enough. She busied herself by spinning crazy stories of her future adventure across the wide ocean. She taught herself to create little animals out of folded towels, and she would leave little paper butterflies and rabbits on the towel rack of the hotel bathrooms. She had to wear her long black hair in a tight bun, and sometimes she pretended that she was a ballerina.

She just wished that she could save the money faster. She was paid almost nothing for her cleaning work.

One day, as she was tucking in the ends of the cheap bed sheet that covered the mattress, a square-faced businessman with rough skin opened the door to the room.

"I'm sorry," she said meekly. "I'm almost done." She went to the bathroom to get the basket that she used to haul her cleaning supplies from room to room. She heard a loud *click* and felt an instant, jarring premonition of danger. She took a deep breath. Everything was fine, she assured herself.

When she emerged from the bathroom, the businessman was sitting on the bed. The door was closed. He'd locked it. He was undoing his belt.

She quickly tried to run past him to unlock the door and leave. Almost lazily, he caught the end of her uniform and held it so she couldn't reach the door. Her heart felt like it was about to fall out of her mouth. She could hear only the blood pounding in her ears. She started screaming. She screamed as he tore her clothes open. She screamed until she had no voice left. She wasn't sure whether it took minutes or whether it took days. Afterwards, he threw her out of the room without a second look. The door slammed, leaving her crouched over and bleeding in the dirty hallway, with her old mops and sponges scattered across the floor.

She was fourteen. She was drenched with sweat. Blood dripped down her legs. She willed herself the strength to get to an empty hotel room, where she locked the door and gathered herself together in the bathroom. She wiped the blood from her skin. She combed her hair with her fingers. She straightened her clothes, tying her apron over the rip in her dress. Her face was unrecognizable in the mirror, slack and suddenly asymmetric and unresponsive. She looked at herself without seeing anything until she realized that she was bleeding onto the floor.

There were still five hours left in her shift. It didn't matter—she knew she'd never be able to come back to the hotel.

She left her cleaning supplies in the closet and walked stiffly, trying not to limp or cry out, all the way home. She told her mother that she was experiencing terrible cramps, and she went to her bedroom. She laid down, eyes wide open, staring at nothing. She couldn't tell anyone. The shame would be too cruel to her parents. The neighbors would call her a whore. Her family would have to abandon her. Then what would she do? Her only choice was to not tell anyone.

That night, and for many nights afterwards, she couldn't sleep.

My mother told me that story constantly during my own childhood in Hong Kong. I was eight years old when I first heard the details of her brutal rape in the hotel. Our family lived between a bar and a brothel, so perhaps this was my mother's real-life boogeyman story to keep me vigilant against the men who were constantly prowling around the hallways and stairs. And it wasn't just at home that we needed to be cautious. Whenever we walked around the market or the bustling main streets, my mother guarded us carefully, seeing rapists and predators where other people saw street vendors and businessmen. She used our neighborhood as a cautionary tale. "This is why you have to get to America," she told my sister and me as she dreamed of this faraway utopia.

My mother did her best to put us on the right path. She exposed us to different, more gracious worlds, expanding our environment through the venues available to us. Wanting us to understand the world beyond Hong Kong, she carved out a place for us in a lovely Catholic mission school where all the classes were held in English, where some teachers came from

Europe to teach us literature and foreign languages, and the nuns taught us about the great God above us. At the expense of many other things, my parents even enrolled our family in a country club. This strange luxury provided a better social education than I could have found anywhere else. I saw the club members as just people, each with dreams in their hearts. We hid our poverty well. My mother was a clever and artful seamstress, and could copy designer clothes for cheap. As a child I learned early to live simultaneously in contradictory but parallel worlds, meeting expatriate children at a country club and then coming home to greet my neighbors: the waiters and prostitutes. To each other they were different, but to me they were people just trying to make it in a city with millions.

This early exposure to all economic groups shaped me. I learned that life at every income level carries broken dreams and heartaches. I learned that the pain of upper-class loneliness could feel just as terrible as the pain of physical hunger.

But my life of contradictions made me fearful, too. I knew what life could be if I made it into what I saw as the upper echelon; I also knew what life could be if I failed. As a child, I hated my mother's story of poverty, begging, and trauma. I hated it *so much*. As my parents struggled to provide basic necessities, both physical and emotional, I made it my goal to one day walk into a store and buy whatever I wanted. I swore that I would never live like my mother, and I worked tirelessly in search of a way out.

Even as a child, I could see that her efforts to rise above her beginnings had dead-ended in this cramped apartment, where we squeezed into two rooms while renting out the other two to make ends meet. She was attached to a husband who doted on her one day, then vented his anger and frustration on her as they struggled to keep up with expenses. Her lack of education was a constant reminder that she was unable to earn a decent wage. No matter how much distance she put between her and the day she scratched on the door of a disgruntled aunt, she was still begging for each bowl of rice.

But my life will be different from my mother's, I told myself as a teenager, when I won a scholarship to attend college in America. I saw how my mother had few options without education and I pursued getting my degrees with vengeance.

Upon graduating with an MBA, I received several job offers and chose the one that gave me the most income. I was convinced that lack of income killed my mother's spirit and I was determined never to put myself in the same predicament. When my husband and I had our two sons, our household was stable and financially secure. I wanted everything my mother ever wanted for me. Yet with all the outward embellishment of success, it was easy enough to ignore the feelings of sorrow and emptiness that sometimes overtook me completely.

I never expected to give up my paycheck and financial independence I received from corporate America. But when my first son was diagnosed with asthma at nine months old, I felt compelled to become a stay-at-home mother to oversee his care, a job I found as challenging and isolating as my 85-hour workweeks at Booz Allen and Hamilton. My time at home led me to conclude that since God is my creator, surely

He has the answers for my life. I started seriously studying God's Word in an attempt to find whatever it was I knew I was missing. I heard an ad on the radio announcing an extension site for Dallas Theological Seminary in Houston and felt compelled to apply. When I was accepted and was attending my first class I turned in my homework assignments, not realizing my professor was adjunct faculty who had agreed to teach one class while serving as President of a different Bible College. Without telling me, this professor had saved a copy of my work as a sample of a perfect assignment. When there was a need in the Bible College he was over, he called to say that while planning on bringing in additional personnel, my homework had fallen out of his files. Tongue in cheek, he said I was God's answer to his prayers and invited me to be interviewed. During that same time I had prayed, "God, if you want to use my life in full time ministry, I would really like to work with people of all ethnicities." Because I knew the Bible College reached a multi ethnic student body, I felt sure my answer to the job offer was yes though I was unsure what I would be doing. Within a short time, I found myself assisting in several areas resulting in a promotion to Vice President of Special Programs. As part of my responsibilities I was asked to organize a citywide women's conference to inspire women across the city from every ethnic community to serve at their potential. I never expected I would be offered the invitation to take my favorite initiative and grow it independently, into a nonprofit of its own.

I didn't have nonprofit training. I certainly hadn't spent my whole life dreaming about doing this work. But the door that opened was *so right*, this idea of a new and singular organization for women of all ethnicities and economic levels—

women who hungered to know their purpose, or who needed scholarships for education and resources for their own out-reach work. There was such an enormous need for an organization that cared about a woman's dreams to effect change in the world.

But could I bring myself to be dependent on charity? I wondered, pausing at the crossroads. Every bone in my body resisted this business model. Nonprofit work meant trusting other people to provide every penny needed to carry out our mission. I felt terrified. I kept thinking about my mother's words, which she'd heard from her own mother: "You know who your real friends are when you have to beg for a bowl of rice."

With my childhood shaped by my mother's story, does it surprise you that I have never felt well prepared for new beginnings, especially one that required me to be dependent on others?

Maybe there are other women out there like this—women who fear change, because they are still searching for stable roots. Maybe you're like this too. I was drawn to corporate life because it gave me a well-defined niche and a finite, predictable job description. I had believed in God since I was a child, but I had never dreamed of placing *all* my hopes in Him in this way. I wasn't sure if I could trust God to be sufficient when I was still wrestling with the many ways my mother had fallen, utterly alone, with no one to help her, not even the God she believed in.

But I chose the nonprofit. I chose Inspire Women. I chose to accept the reality that I had always resisted: that God had been targeting my deepest vulnerabilities in the process of showing me my greatest calling. I stopped allowing my emotional baggage to hold me hostage from what could be. I threw myself into the nonprofit, without a safety net, without a headquarters, without anything in the bank. All I had was the mission God placed in my path and a conviction that I had no other choice but to build it.

And, if you can believe it, everything followed from there in time.

Of course, founding Inspire Women meant that my mother's story began to reappear in my life, day after day. A few months after operations had begun to settle down, I distributed a survey to all the women who requested scholarships. I discovered that 60% of them came from backgrounds of abuse, and 40% of them came from churches that did not have the funds to invest in the potential of women to serve their communities. I found that even the privileged women who gave to the ministry struggled with needs—not for the basics, but for self-actualization, a struggle which felt just as painful as any other. Many of the women I encountered reminded me of my mother, or the women I had met at the country club who hungered for a voice and an identity. My mother's words—laments, tales of pain, frustrated dreams, and lost battles to overcome circumstances that suffocated her potential—began to ring through my head once more.

Confronting her life all over again was a painful process. I had spent my twenties crippled by my mother's suicide and my thirties avoiding the sadness that overcame me whenever I thought about it. I thought I had moved on, but as I began working with these women, the fullness of my mother's tragedy was resurrected in a way that was more immediate than ever. I saw her face, her broken heart, in every woman I met who had come from a background of poverty, trauma, or abuse, or who simply had a dream that was yet to be fulfilled.

There are so many women like my mother—like me—who were never allowed to be children, who have never known an unburdened life.

Unexpectedly, I found threads of redemption within even the most desperate stories. I saw alternative possibilities for my mother's life. I began grieving not for the terrible things that had happened, but for all of the beautiful things that she had rendered impossible by taking her own life. In this, I was led to the peace that gave me purpose within my ministry and within my personal relationship with God and community.

Today, Inspire Women inspires thousands of women at a gathering that reflects the world God intended—where there are no artificial barriers between ethnicities and economic levels; where women are equally empowered to reach their potential; and where women can apply for funding for scholarships and ministry grants. From these friends and fellow sojourners, I have learned that there is always a path to resilience and healing from past stories, no matter the pain that has come before. Our past can fuel our future.

One day, someone called me a "motherless daughter" and I bristled. I don't like labels like this, which seem to imply that I am somehow a lesser person for the years that I have lacked my mother's love. We are not reducible to the tragedies that we have experienced. The story never ends there.

The same goes for our mothers. They are more than their traumas, their failures, and their inabilities to provide. Many women in this world have this in common: we only knew our mothers as shells of their former selves. We knew their coping mechanisms but not their true hopes and passions, not their dreams that died along the hard and unpredictable path of life.

These dreams can be resurrected. There are millions of women out there, mothers and daughters both, who have survived hell—so it's never too late to start rebuilding.

But what about my mother? Her story hangs heavy over my head as I write this. For her, it will always be too late. She set all of her dreams aside and pinned her last hopes on her daughters making it to America. Then once our place in the free country was secure, our mother felt she had nothing left to live for.

Her death is even more tragic in light of the fact that she could have come to America herself, to join us, less than two years after we made the journey. Our father's application for permanent residence was approved in 1976.

Had she not grown so desperate, she would have found that even for her—a woman who had known nothing but limitations and poverty since childhood—there was hope, there was promise, there was the chance for change and renewal.

There are no fairytale stories in this book. But there are extraordinary threads of hope in the chapters that follow. Together we'll learn how to fight off the past and live freely within the lives we still have a chance to shape.

With our faith in a great God who can transform our suffering we will make sense of our suffering and find our unique voice to change the world.

CHAPTER 2

✦

Hope Rises and Falls

At fourteen, my mother thought her life was over and done. Female purity was an obsessive priority in Chinese culture. She knew that she could never be wed to a Chinese man. She accepted her likely fate—to be single for the rest of her life.

She withdrew even more into her mind. Once a week or so, she felt the urge to return to school. The urge was so powerful that she daydreamed about books and homework; however, she needed to continue working to support her family. She found a new job at a tea shop, washed dishes for eight-hour stretches at a time, wondering what a single woman could possibly do with her life in Shanghai.

Families often came into the tea shop with young children. The sound of the kids playing and babbling would float through the kitchen window to reach my mother's ears. Hearing them, she thought about how children were so innocent and full of energy, like puppies trusting to be fed. She would never have the chance to guard that state of wonder in her own children. She would never get to protect a son or a daughter.

The long days of grimy teacups and angry cooks passed and blended into each other. The seasons changed. Every hour that passed, my mother worked to keep one question at bay: *why, why, why had no one protected her?*

Just a few miles away from the neighborhood where my mother worked in her storefront tea shop, the young metropolis that was Shanghai in the 1940's was expanding and remaking itself into a city that was bustling, decadent, and wildly diverse. It was the financial center of China, the largest port city, and the center of many cultural industries like publishing, film, and opera. Newly built roads crossed the city like veins, transporting an unending and fabulous parade of carts carrying bright silks, hulking bags of fragrant tea, and intricately painted porcelain vases. Art Deco buildings rose on every corner. Chinese bankers walked the streets wearing expensive suits. British, French, and American expats mingled in dark, elegant corners of bars where dice flew on tabletops and gorgeous women offered them cigarettes that tasted somehow Continental.

But no one in Shanghai forgot who the city really belonged to: the Japanese. The city had fallen to foreign control in 1937, during the Second Sino-Japanese War. The Japanese would ultimately occupy the city for eight years. Before the Japanese occupancy, the Chinese government had welcomed all foreigners including Jews from Europe with no passport or visa necessary. This policy shaped Shanghai into a strange new territory. During World War II—in which the Second Sino-Japanese War became our Pacific battlefront—as countries all over the world shut their doors to the panicking Jewish citizens of Europe, Shanghai was one of only two places in the world that stayed unconditionally open to Jewish immigrants. Consequently, there was an overwhelming migration of European Jews, coming to the Eastern city from Baghdad and Russia and France, with talent and connections and culture to spare.

One of these Jews was a thirty-four-year-old blond named James Jonassen, trained as a lawyer in Germany. As far as he knew, he was the only one of his family to have escaped Germany. He arrived in Shanghai in early 1939 with no connections, no ability to speak Chinese, and no idea what to do.

He had come to China by a surreal, luxurious steamship, commandeered by a rogue Italian diplomat who was in the business of smuggling Western European Jews to safety. There had been hundreds of Germans on the ship, but no one that James knew. He had spent most of the voyage in his tiny bedchamber, seasick and worried for his family, who had been nowhere to be found when James managed to hustle a ticket for himself on the boat.

There was nothing to do but move forward. Through an acquaintance he had met during the journey, James Jonassen managed to rent a two-floor apartment building in the southwest quadrant of Shanghai. He lived sparingly on the second floor, leaving the first floor—a vacant space that had once been a restaurant—empty. Soon, he was overwhelmed by the amount of free time in his life. Entrepreneurial by nature, James was too disciplined and sober in temperament to feel at ease in the opulent nightclubs where most other Europeans gathered to drink and look at showgirls. He hunted around the streets of Shanghai until he found a store on West Nanjing Road that sold paint and brushes and other tools. He fixed up the restaurant, adding stylish dark blue trim to the counters and walls. He went to his favorite local cafe and, with the help of his English-speaking landlord, offered the second-in-command cook a job that would pay double.

They called the restaurant Paris of the Orient. James filled it with framed advertisements of beautiful cigarette girls, all Chinese women in long sleek dresses, always clutching something cute and tiny: a fur stole, a kitten, a perfect fat tulip. His chef was skeptical about these decorations, and although he tried to persuade James to put fine Chinese art on the walls instead, the German man held steady. He liked the cigarette ads. The girls in them reminded him of German movie stars and made him feel at home.

The restaurant didn't take off right away. James, undaunted, asked his cook to improve the recipes for drunken chicken and lacquered duck. He tinkered himself with the wonton recipes until they resembled the dumplings that his grandmother had once made for him at her country house. In the meantime, he put an advertisement outside the building asking for a Chinese tutor. He figured he might as well keep busy, and the language skills would help him in his business.

One day, a lively sixteen-year-old girl walked in—my mother.

"Chinese teacher?" she asked, in accented English. "I'm best Chinese teacher." She had practiced those words over and over again, praying that it would help her snag the position. She hadn't worked for a few weeks and the family was on the brink of going hungry again.

James looked at the girl. Her black hair was tied back in a ponytail and she had a nervous smile on her face. She was so beautiful. She also looked hungry. He called the chef out from the back room, where he had been smoking cigarettes inside the kitchen despite James' constant admonitions to stop.

"Hey Lee, let's have some chicken and rice," he said. He turned to my mother. "I'm pretty old—I might be a slow learner."

She smiled widely, feeling a flood of adrenaline. She had the job! "You learn Chinese very fast and good," she said carefully.

"How do I introduce myself to you?" he asked.

"What is the name?"

"James," he said, gesturing to a table and pulling out a chair.

"Wo shi James," she said. (Translated, this meant "I am James")

"Wo shi James," he repeated, looking into the girl's dark eyes.

My mother fell quietly in love with this man, who treated her differently than anyone she had ever met before. He was always pulling out chairs for her and asking her how her food tasted. He even brought her plates and chopsticks and refilled her rice, an act which disturbed my mother at first—a man, serving rice to a woman?—but soon seemed incredibly kind.

And there was something about the way that he said her name. It took my mother weeks to figure it out, but finally she realized that he was saying her name as if it were a title, as if it were a designation of respect.

She'd never once in her life felt *respected* before.

As a girl, my mother was quick and brilliant with languages. Although she hadn't been to school since age nine, she'd learned English from the boy in the restaurant she met years ago who was determined to reach America, the one she thought she would one day marry. She'd kept it up by studying newspapers and eavesdropping on conversations at work. James was not as skilled with Chinese, but he was a good and conscientious student. He was better at speaking the language than writing it, and so the two of them began shifting their lessons to simple conversation practice, during which my mother's English rapidly became fluent.

Weeks passed by. My mother began dressing as nicely as she could for their tutoring sessions, which stretched from an hour to two hours to four. Sometimes James would be called away from their lessons by an influx of customers, and my mother watched with almost maternal pride—ridiculous, she thought, since James was almost twenty years her senior—as her student conversed, eagerly although imperfectly, with his Chinese patrons.

She began coming home later in the evening, full of energy. She smiled as she did the thankless chores that fell to her around the house. Her mother looked at her with suspicion, as her young daughter handed over more money than she'd ever made before as a maid or kitchen's helper. "You be careful," my grandmother spat out. "One day he might ask you to do more than teach him Chinese."

At this my mother felt a defiant, glorious thought run through her mind. "Maybe I would do more than teach him Chinese anyway! Maybe one day I'll marry him!" she imagined saying to her mother. She didn't, of course; she merely nodded and went back to her bedroom. All the while she was thinking about how she felt so safe with James, safer than she could ever remember. He talked to her with such compassion and care. He'd asked all about her childhood, and as she told him about her grandfather's funeral, with all the eggs and chickens, she'd begun to feel that James reminded her of that gracious and wise man.

One day, James asked her an odd question, in English. "Where do you see yourself in the future?"

"How many years in the future?" she replied.

"Five years," he said. "I don't know. What are your goals?"

"My *goals?* I don't have goals," she said, the kindness of his question overwhelming her. "You know, I have four younger siblings, and my father hasn't had a job in years..." She felt her stomach knot up. She was still young, and there were still nights where she went to sleep dreaming of a life as a famous actress or a writer of plays. But when she woke up and looked around her, she saw nothing but a life that was closing in, that had been closed in since that day in the hotel, or since the day her grandfather died.

"But you're so smart," James said to her kindly. "And you're still so young. You have a beautiful life ahead of you."

At these words, my mother felt a tear drop down her cheek, then another. She choked out, "Excuse me," and then ran back through the kitchen to the garbage area behind the restaurant. Without looking at her surroundings she sat down on a crate and cried helplessly for this life James imagined for her—a life that she knew she would never have. When she looked up, she saw James standing in the doorway with a sad look on his face.

"I am really sorry to upset you," he said. "I apologize. I am so sorry."

"Things are very different for Chinese girls," she said to him shakily. "And I should not be crying. I am sorry too."

He extended his hand to her and helped her up. "There's nothing you should be sorry for."

She started crying again, her hand still in his. He squeezed her small palm. "I mean it. You're extraordinary."

"What does it mean?" she asked, sniffling, trying to regain her composure.

"Extra," he said, "meaning *more*. You know ordinary. What I mean is that you are *more* than ordinary girls. You're stronger, smarter. Has no one ever told you that? I hope I'm not offending you. I just want you to understand that you deserve to be happy and to have the life that you want. And the world is changing, you know. You can have these things if you want to."

My mother couldn't believe the words she was hearing.

A week later, James asked her to marry him. In a blaze of happiness, she said yes.

Everything happened quickly. James came to her house to formally ask her parents for her hand, an evening that had my mother trembling with anxiety and embarrassment. Her parents, overwhelmed by James's aura of intelligence and kindness and sheer German-ness, barely spoke; her mother gestured at small plates of Chinese delicacies and looked at the couple with a strange expression that mixed confusion, joy, fear, and concern. Everyone in the family made it quite clear that what my mother was doing would mean an excommunication. It was not acceptable to marry a foreigner. It would not be seen favorably in Chinese society. It would make my mother look like one of the showgirls in the clubs, who birthed half-white babies that played in the back rooms while their parents cavorted in finery up front.

"I don't care!" my mother said. "He *loves me*. And we'll never be hungry again!"

They were married at the magistrate's office one summer day. That night, my mother was shaky and anxious with the memory of what had happened at the hotel, with the fear that somehow James would know she had been compromised. Yet James, sensing her discomfort, kissed her sweetly on the neck and shoulder and told her that he wouldn't pressure her into doing anything she didn't want to. Days later, when my mother felt ready, James' gentle and sensitive face kept her mind from sliding back into the horrors of the hotel.

The restaurant got busier. James kept up with his Chinese lessons and doted on his new wife. He bought her expensive magazines and fine dresses. He brought home fresh, exotic flowers that my mother had never seen before. They were blissfully happy. For the first few weeks that she spent in the apartment above the restaurant, my mother experienced such giddiness when she

33

woke up that she began pinching her fingertips to remind herself that it was all as real as the sun in the sky.

By 1943, Jewish immigration to Shanghai had reached a critical mass. Poles, Lithuanians, Austrians, Germans, Czechs, Italians, Hungarians, and more; by Italian ferry, by Japanese cruise ship, by land caravans across Siberia and secret passages arranged by fearless ambassadors, they'd streamed into Shanghai until all in all, there were 18,000 Jews in the young, unstable, cosmopolitan city.

Well—18,000 and a half, if you counted a two-year-old boy named Bobby Jonassen, a curious and intelligent toddler who had my mother's eyes and a blond streak in his hair from his father. My mother and her husband delighted in Bobby's every move, allowing him to bang all the pots in the kitchen and invent all of his own names for the things he saw.

Then, the Japanese army issued an edict. All Jews in the city who had immigrated after 1937 had to relocate to the Hongkew district, a small and impoverished quarter of the city where group homes sprouted in the dirt like mushrooms. They called it "Little Vienna," in reference to the Austrian refugees who had already moved in. Little Vienna, which was less than one square mile in size, would have to hold 100,000 Chinese citizens as well as the majority of the Jewish population in Shanghai. The recently immigrated Jews had only three months to move.

The officials of Shanghai worried about the consequences of this forced relocation. Everyone hoped that the Chinese citizens of Hongkew would leave as their neighborhood was given over to the coerced foreigners—but as the Jews were brought in, none of the Chinese showed any signs of vacating their apartments. With no buildings emptied, thousands and thousands of Jews were packed into an abandoned elementary school and a cluster of dirty apartments where they had to sleep ten to a room.

James Jonassen was one of the last men in Shanghai to enter Little Vienna, which by then was called the Shanghai Ghetto. He had stayed quiet for the first two months after the edict was pronounced, living under the radar as hundreds of European Jews trudged into the cordoned-off quarters of the war camp. He'd hoped against reason that he could stay hidden in his restaurant for the rest of the war, safe and anonymous with his family.

But the big German owner of the oddly named restaurant—who could forget a name like Paris of the Orient?—was a well-known figure in the neighborhood. It was only a matter of time. Still, James kept holding on, gazing upon his wife and child as if he could absorb them into his body, as if he could take them with him into that unknown place.

After a few weeks, when the Japanese soldiers began patrolling the streets and posting documents about the fierce penalties faced by any "stateless persons" if they did not move to the Ghetto, my mother became frantic with anxiety. Every night she wept, overwhelmed by her husband's impending confinement.

"What if they kill you?" she sobbed, the day the inevitable moment arrived.

James sighed. The inevitable had arrived. "Keep running the restaurant without me, okay?" he said to his wife.

35

He kissed his young son on the cheek. "You're going to be so grown-up when I get back, Bobby."

The next day, he walked to the Hongkew district and was herded into a filthy apartment with mildew creeping down the walls, no furniture, and a dozen Jews of all ages sprawled out on the floor, making plans to help this make-shift community survive the war. James sat down, feeling despondent. He'd hoped to be able to sneak out during the day and help run the restaurant, but these thoughts had disappeared as soon as he saw the heavily manned fence that would keep them within the Ghetto until the Japanese army was ready to let them out. There would be no work for any of these European Jews, no help with the broken plumbing, no schooling for their children, no pharmacies open to cure their ills. The people in James' apartment were making dismal jokes about the Japanese rations that were distributed to them twice a day.

James saw that the refugees would have to do it all themselves—to build a new life from scratch in a foreign land, for the second time in just a few years. They needed to establish a list of doctors among them, a market system, a method of distributing social services. They needed to make an alliance with the Chinese people who still shared this small corner of Shanghai. "I speak a little Chinese," he said to his new roommates. "What do you need help with?"

Over the next few months, as the industrious and defiant refugees managed to create a little society within their prison, James thought of his wife and son every hour, every minute. Other refugees were allowed day passes out of the camp to go to school, or to work. But the Japanese were especially suspicious of the German Jews, and the guards especially disliked James Jonassen. His wife and son weren't allowed to visit, and he wasn't allowed to leave. He settled for writing letters—only a few of which were ever delivered and which my mother read over and over until they disintegrated.

At first, my mother was strong. She managed the restaurant, hired an additional cook, and doted on Bobby, the son of her dream marriage. But with every passing day without James, she sensed life was about to change and there was nothing she could do to stop it.

The winter of 1943 came, bitter and unrelenting. Reports came floating back from the Shanghai Ghetto that the Jews within were dying of hunger and frostbite. The city seemed encased in a layer of dirty ice. My mother closed the restaurant one day for good. She walked the few miles back to her old neighborhood, where her mother, father, and siblings still lived. Though they hadn't seen her since Bobby's birth, they greeted her not with joy but with cruelty.

"So high and mighty, Miss Germany," her mother said. "And now you've returned because you can't feed your own son."

Hearing this, my mother wanted to scream. Hadn't she sacrificed her whole life in that hotel so her younger brothers and sisters wouldn't go hungry? Instead, she handed her mother a wallet with a moderate amount of money. "It's not that I can't feed my son. It's that I want him to know the rest of his family, now that we don't know what might happen to his father."

Everyone was skeptical of Bobby, who looked noticeably different from the rest of the family. But as the winter went on, Bobby's grandmother began to grudgingly accept her half-white grandson—so clever with the puzzles and games that his mother created for him. As he began to use words and even complete sentences, he spoke Chinese with a slight German accent, a sound that everyone found charming—everyone except for my mother, who would sometimes have to leave the room to avoid publicly being engulfed in tears, reminded of the husband she missed.

In the meantime, the Shanghai Ghetto was declining. The Jewish residents made friends with the Chinese families of the neighborhood, who sometimes cooked meals for them and cared for the sick children. But what little money they had was disappearing, and the winter had taken its toll. Some Jews were getting dangerously involved in intelligence efforts to subvert their Japanese captors, which resulted in a painful crackdown. The guards continued to show an active distrust towards James Jonassen and the rest of the Germans. Months went by when no one was allowed to leave, and health conditions worsened.

When winter began to thaw into spring, my mother—near-crazed by fear that James was dead—began taking daily walks around the perimeter of the camp, pacing as close to the enclosure as she could without facing chastisement from the Japanese guards. She brought Bobby, putting him on her shoulders or carrying him on her back when he grew too tired to walk. Through the tarps and fences of the enclosure she could see flashes of people, glimpses of their faces, and sometimes her heart raced when she thought she might have caught a glimpse of her husband.

Once, she happened to be at the front gate while the guards were changing shifts. They were squabbling over something and barely looking at the entrance to the Ghetto. My mother quickly seized the opportunity to walk in, grabbing Bobby and carrying him on her hip as she strode as quickly as she could without running.

"What are you doing, woman?" a guard shouted behind her as she moved to swiftly create distance between them.

"I live here!" she said, tossing the words over her shoulder nonchalantly. The guards nodded, distracted, and returned to their disagreement.

My mother's heart filled with joy and fear as she continued to walk. She stopped into the shops and the community center to inquire about a German man named James Jonassen. "He's tall," she said, barely holding back her tears.

One old woman led her to a health clinic, where James was sorting through paperwork. When he saw my mother, his face changed, like a cloud had been lifted. He opened his arms and embraced her silently, for what felt like hours. He picked up his son and wouldn't let him go.

They spent that day together, publicly huddled in the waiting room of the clinic. They didn't eat, they didn't drink tea, they didn't care who saw them crying and laughing and just looking at each other.

"Your legs look swollen," my mother said to James, as he leaned over to scratch a mosquito bite on his calf. He waved her remark away. "A lot of people here have this. It's fine. I feel fine."

Bobby, copying his father as he'd always done, crossed his legs and scratched at an imaginary bump. "I FEEL FINE!" he howled blissfully.

When the sun started to go down, my mother had to leave. "I'll come back and see you as soon as I can," she said, staying composed. "I love you."

The next dozen times my mother tried to enter the Shanghai Ghetto, she was turned away. "We know who you are, woman," the guards said to her. "You're married to that German." Months went by, as my mother tried to change her hairstyle and dress, all to no avail. Having Bobby with her made it hard for her to be anonymous. Still, she kept bringing her baby, hoping to provide James with an opportunity to see his son.

Then, one boiling hot summer day, a guard told her flatly that James Jonassen was dead. The word hit my mother like an anvil. The guard laughed at her shock and slammed the gate in her face.

My mother couldn't be sure if the guard was telling the truth. She walked away from the camp, holding Bobby's little hands. He said, "Dada?"

"Dada will come back one day," she said to her son. He didn't say another word. He had always had a certain understanding of how things worked. At home he took all his toys apart and reassembled them thoughtfully, as if he understood that all of life could break into small pieces.

My mother was never again allowed in the Ghetto. She began to feel as if that one day with James had been a dream.

Little Bobby, over time, started to forget his father. He'd begun calling his favorite toy "Dada," which did not amuse my mother one bit.

There was no way to know which air raid killed James Jonassen. There was no way to know if it was an air raid at all, really. It could have been sickness or hunger or any number of things. The only thing that we know is that, when the Shanghai Ghetto was finally opened after the war, James Jonassen never walked out.

Picture my mother—slim and youthful, not even twenty years of age—with her long black braid down her back and wearing her best blue dress, waiting anxiously by the Ghetto gates. By this time, she's holding the hand of a three-year-old boy whose blond streak had almost completely disappeared. Thin and pallid Jews are streaming out of the doors of the compound and my mother's heart is pounding, her body filling with adrenaline at every tall man she sees. She stays at the gates of the compound all day and all night, until there's no one left except for a few guards, until she can see nothing but dirty buildings and the refuse of a war camp that people were already starting to forget.

There's no way to know what killed James Jonassen.

By the end of that day, my mother felt like a walking ghost. She headed home in pitch darkness with her son Bobby on her back, wondering if there were any mercies left in this city.

My mother didn't often speak about this period in her life. There were gaps in her story—perhaps because they were better forgotten than kept alive—where she would risk opening old wounds and from which she might never recover.

I suspect that James' memory sustained her through the hard years to come. By the time she gave birth to my sister and me, she had closed that chapter. She only ever mentioned her short, surreal years with James in moments of extreme frustration—moments when she had to remind herself that whatever sorrows life had brought her, at least she'd once been married to a man who treated her like a queen.

Her relationship with my father was very different. With the two of them, romance and passion mixed with rage and verbal assault. Under the weight of the pressure he'd put on himself, my father dumped his anger on my mother whenever money was short. My mother—anything but submissive, despite the cultural norms of her time and place— would pour fuel right back on the fire. The fights would escalate to a breaking point, and my mother always broke first. She didn't have the emotional reserves to cope and recover, so she would retreat like a wounded animal, hiding in a corner of the house to cry quietly in her pain and humiliation.

I was close to my mother—much closer than my sister, who was sporty and brusque, like my father. So, when my mother cried, I felt like I was hurting too. I'd go to her, wherever she was hiding, and try to console her. Damp-faced and flushed, she would tell me, "Never let a man dump on you like this. I want you to grow up to be strong. Study hard and learn to support yourself. When you can't feed yourself, you give other people too much power over you."

Years later, I remember asking my father why he was so harsh to my mother. His answer surprised me. "Did you ever hear the words she spoke to me?" he asked. As a child, it never occurred to me that perhaps my father's heart was crushed as well. All I saw was that my mother felt second-class. Hearing her talk about men and marriage added one more thing to my list of goals: to make enough money to support myself all my life. As I saw it, dependence equaled weakness; weakness meant setting yourself up to be hurt.

I made the mistake of thinking of my parents as caregivers only, rather than people with dreams of their own. It was a long time before I could understand that my mother was a woman before and after she was a mother—that her time with James was the only time that she slipped into a world of indulgence, frolicking in freedom and in happiness, and the life that followed was a stark contrast that continually reminded her of what she had lost.

Perhaps because of this blissful first marriage, she, like so many women I've met in my life—like me, once upon a time—spent years laboring under the idea that the right man would fix and perfect her life. As her second marriage became increasingly combative, she set her sights upward—to a God who had the power to stay, who would never die or fail her. Her innocent faith led her to pray constantly, embracing the idea of Him as her new, ultimate Prince Charming. He was the only one who could save her.

This belief changed her and gave her new strength. She never read the Bible, but she always seemed to be brimming with stories of God and deliverance that she memorized from Sunday mass. Her ironclad, mysterious sense of the divine filled her with hope. She believed that the

God who carried her from Shanghai to Hong Kong and sustained her would make a way for the family in America. The key, as she saw it, was to get to a free land. "Get the foundation solid and then the rest will follow," she told me, in moments of determination. "If you don't, it will only be a matter of time before the house crumbles."

My father feared the idea of going to America, not believing that we would be allowed to go, fearing that we wouldn't be able to survive there. My mother couldn't stand this cautiousness. If it hadn't been for my sister and me, I think my mother would have walked out just to show my father she could. But she stayed with us, stayed with her dreams, although she now believed them to be beyond the reach of any human Prince Charming. Because God was the only knight remaining, she begged Him to come through for her and her daughters. She did not know how He would do it, she just knew that He surely would—that the God she believed in would ride into her life on a shining, perfect horse and set all things right.

No wonder it crushed her when her plans for America seemed finally doomed. When U.S. Immigration rejected my mother and father's petition to go to America while her children were granted student visas, did she feel she had taken us to an open door but the door then slammed in her face? On the blackest of nights in my first years in America, I would find myself thinking about my mother's thoughts in those confusing, panic-filled final days before her death. Was she offering her death as a penance? Was she hoping that God would exchange her life for our safety? She had always sacrificed for her family. Perhaps she didn't know what else to do, other than to try—one last time—to offer herself up for the ones she loved.

I couldn't bring myself to think much about this until recently. For many years, I could only see my mother's suicide through the lens of myself. I dwelled on the way she had abandoned me, the way she had given up on her daughters, the way she had passed her brokenness down to me.

Then I grew up and took myself out of the center of my thoughts. I realized that, throughout her arduous life, my mother fought and overcame so many brutal circumstances that attacked her at every turn. The demons on the outside were not what destroyed her—it was the demons on the inside. She did the best with what she was given.

The child in me still doesn't know why God didn't send her a message, or some last reserve of strength, that would assure her that she could trust Him. Faith seems to be something God desired from my mother and desires from me. He will not eliminate the need for faith in our lives—in any of our lives.

Still, I wish that my mother had a community—that she had a close friend to speak her dreams back to her when she forgot them. In looking for God on her own, she forgot that God uses people as His hands and feet. She forgot that this is how God expresses His mercy in a tangible way—through other people, through friends who love us.

It's easy to forget this. It's easy to keep all your burdens to yourself, or even to seek just one relationship as the solution to all things. After all, our world is one that teaches women to wait for an ultimate Prince Charming. And of course, if you've found your earthly prince—over 30 years of marriage makes me pretty sure that I have found mine—

then that's terrific. It's wonderful to have someone to count on. It's wonderful to have one person in your life who represents your safe place, who holds your heart in their hands.

Still, we weren't meant to be sustained by one all-encompassing relationship in life. We need roots, and we need authentic friendships. We thrive best when we serve our purpose in a community. When we give ourselves away to just one person or to one family, our world has become too small. And when our world gets too small, something inside us starts to stir, reminding us that we were created for something bigger.

My mother's decision to give up just before the blessing is what drives me to help women to never abandon their dreams. I have learned from her life. I don't advocate wishful thinking. I don't advocate passivity while waiting for an earthly Prince to come; rather, I advocate believing in the dreams God gives us as our spiritual inheritance, and encouraging each other to fight hard and patiently for our dreams until they become a reality.

God gives us dreams to advance His purpose. Even when dreams are lost, He can make something new out of nothing, the same way He breathed this world into existence. Though the time for my mother's choices is over, I embrace the time I have on earth to pick differently. I choose love that stays, love that pours out from our friends and relationships. I choose endurance until the finish, and I wholeheartedly acknowledge that I cannot accomplish my dreams, heal my wounds, or understand the real work of God without the presence of true friends around me.

If you've ever had your heart wounded, you may hear a counselor tell you that it takes another person to close and heal that wound. To this day, it still seems almost shockingly simple to me, this basic proof of our need for each other. But it's true. Our wounds can't be truly healed by money or work or going to the gym or escaping on vacation or drinking ourselves into a stupor at the bar. Our wounds from the loss of a loved one can't be healed in solitude; we are better off embracing new friendships and relationships, and seeking God through these blessings.

For all the women out there who are hurting—don't isolate yourself. There are organizations like Inspire Women who will engage you with support and love and friendship. The verse in the Bible that sums up a foundational truth in our universe is this: *It is not good for man to be alone.*

CHAPTER 3

Choices at the Crossroads

My mother was always vague about the period between her first and second marriages, the years that separated the death of James Jonassen in Shanghai and the unlikely whirlwind romance that she found in a bustling port of Hong Kong. I found most of my clues during times of sadness, the moments when losses in my mother's past would resurface, and she would sit at our dinner table with her eyes glassy and pensive.

"Where did she go?" I would wonder, then only six or seven years old. From as far back as I can remember, I knew my mother hid more than she showed. She was a woman with many secrets, who had seemingly lived many lives in her past. But sometimes I was lucky enough to catch her in a moment of openness, when she would share her memories with me.

Frequently, the name Betty emerged from the ashes. From my mother's stories of her one true girlfriend came a narrative of friendship, trust, weakness, hope, and tragedy.

After losing James, my mother spent the autumn of 1945 in a daze. Though she was back to work at another cafe, she couldn't shake the habit of walking in huge, looping circles all across the city, hoping to catch a glimpse of a husband that she couldn't yet fully believe was dead.

So, as the weather changed and the leaves turned red and golden, as the streets of Shanghai shone brightly in the rain, as construction workers carried wheelbarrows of rubble and the city began to regain its legs and life, my mother saw nothing except for her own grief. She just worked and walked, worked and walked. She took Bobby with her nearly every day. Then one day, as the little boy protested against the outing—"My legs are tired, Mama!"—another waitress at the cafe spoke up. "Why don't you leave him with me this afternoon?" she asked.

The young waitress's name was Betty. My mother hadn't taken much notice of her before, but Betty had been watching my mother carefully every day, curious about this girl's life story, her sadness, her youth, and especially her half-white child who was so content to sit at a table in the kitchen and tinker with the same shabby toys all day.

My mother hesitated. "I wouldn't want to impose," she said.

Bobby clapped his hands. "I walk if Betty walks!"

"Well," my mother said, "the kid has spoken. Would you like to come on our walk with us?"

"Sure! Where are we going?" asked Betty.

"Nowhere, really," my mother said. "There's nowhere to go."

Talking for long hours when business was slow and they had nothing to do but roll up the napkins, the two of them became good friends. It turned out that they had much in common. Betty had also come from a hard family background, had also been forced to work since childhood, and was accustomed to being leered at and targeted and smacked by strange men. She had the same decisive energy as my mother, and the two of them bemoaned all of the things that were holding them back in Shanghai. Betty was aghast at my mother's story, once my mother finally got up the courage to tell everything to her new friend.

But my mother wasn't the only girl in the neighborhood who had been raped, and James Jonassen wasn't the only person who had died in the war. Betty approached the situation with a blunt practicality. "We need to get out of here," she said. "I'm serious. Neither of us can be sure of work if we stay here."

Betty had to care for her grandmother on her off days, and she sometimes took Bobby with her, to give my mother a break. One day, Betty was fussing with the radio, which was broadcasting thick white noise, and Bobby—a boy of five—asked to see it. Within a minute, he had tweaked the receiver and fixed it completely. Betty stared at him, then laughed loudly. When my mother came back to fetch him, Betty said, "You've got a little genius on your hands."

My mother's eyes were beginning to open as her friend helped heal her heart. On her daily walks, she heard the whispers of an impending revolution circulating on the streets. She picked up copies of underground newspapers, and read articles warning of unrest and upheaval. Her biggest concern was lack of employment. One day she came across a bulletin from Hong Kong detailing the opportunities that were available there under British rule. She read every word of the bulletin a dozen times, fermenting a plan.

The next day she greeted Betty at the cafe with wide eyes and an aura of determination. "You have a grandmother who needs help. I have a son, and my parents who aren't getting any younger. Neither of us is making any money at the cafe. Do you still want to get out of here?" she asked.

"I always want to get out of here," said Betty.

"Let's go to Hong Kong, then," my mother said. "Let's go as soon as we can."

My mother thought she had a good chance convincing her parents to relocate, since her father was still unable to make good money in Shanghai. "The opportunities in Hong Kong will be so much better," she beseeched them, to no avail. Her family insisted that they were settled. They'd made friends in the neighborhood; there was extended family all around them. They considered the idea of moving to Hong Kong to be completely outlandish.

"If someone doesn't leave China to find work, the family will starve!" my mother pleaded. "It's going to be different here—things will get worse."

"What do you fear about living in China? Things may be just as bad in Hong Kong and we'll have no family there." her mother said. "Stop talking this way. Best to just stay here with family." My mother gritted her teeth, knowing that she was resolved.

Betty was ready to leave at a moment's notice, but there was one thing my mother couldn't figure out: what to do with Bobby. Who would care for him while she worked? Who could she trust in a new city? Betty would be just as busy trying to survive as she would.

"You have to leave Bobby. You just *have* to do it until you can send for him," Betty finally told her bluntly, one night when the two of them were rummaging through Betty's bedroom in search of the few valuables that she might bring on their journey. My mother was sitting on her friend's bed, and she felt a rising panic. She looked at the dingy walls and the ragged old belongings that surrounded her. She started to cry, first timidly, then in uncontrollable sobs.

Betty got up from the floor and sat down on the bed beside her friend. She hugged her, stroking her hair. "We'll come back for him," she said, trying to soothe her friend. "This is the best thing you can do for him right now. Give him a connection to the outside world. Make money for him so that he can leave some day."

My mother's parents didn't like the idea of keeping Bobby, but they liked it better than the idea of Bobby on the road with their young and foolish daughter, headed to a strange city and an uncertain future.

"Oh, well, just another mouth to feed," sighed my grandmother.

"He's not an *animal*," said my mother, close to tears. She'd been inconsolable since she'd made up her mind. "He's such a good boy, Mama. He's so smart and so well-behaved and he's going to do so well for himself. I bet he'll go to America someday and become a businessman."

At this her mother cackled rudely. "Sure! What a nice story. You know, I'll be happy if he eventually just earns his keep."

Earns his keep! My mother remembered her early childhood years of begging and prayed that Bobby would never have to submit himself to that humiliation.

In the week before she left, she took Bobby on longer and longer walks. She told him every detail about his father that she could remember. She told him to study hard in school and to never listen to any negative word the family might say to him about not fitting in. While setting aside the items she would take with her, she found Bobby's baby quilt, which he'd discarded with the assertion that he was a big boy. The quilt was pale blue and filled with soft goose down. She stuck the blanket in her suitcase.

One day, as she was feeling sick about leaving him, she was reminded of an incident from a few years earlier. On one of their walks, Bobby—then just a toddler—had pointed upwards. "Look, Mama, a man!"

My mother looked up and saw nothing but white clouds drifting across the clear, bright sky.

"Man, Mama, man!" insisted Bobby. "In the clouds!"

"I don't see anything, little bear," she said to her son.

Bobby smiled contentedly. "I see man."

They had spent the rest of the walk in silence. That day, my mother wondered if Bobby had felt something divine—if he had sensed, in his childish mind, a connection to the world that lies beyond what we can see, the world where his father was. As they walked, he smiled at nothing, busy in his own thoughts. Looking at him, my mother had felt a vague but tenacious hope that God's favor was with Bobby. As she thought about this day, she etched the memory on her heart. She vowed to remember this and take comfort in it. She felt, again, that Bobby would make it. He would somehow be protected in her absence.

However, her hope of God's blessing on Bobby did little to help her the day she had to board the train and say goodbye. She poked her head out the window as the dust and steam billowed all around her, smiling at him through her tears and flailing her arms outside the train for as long as she dared. It was early morning and Bobby stood sleepy and composed and tall for his age—her last connection to happiness, left behind on a train platform in Shanghai. She tried to convince herself that he was not a toddler anymore. Wasn't he a young man by now? But it was no use trying to fool herself. Really, she knew he was a seven-year-old whom she had forced to grow up overnight. She stuck her hand in her suitcase and pulled out Bobby's baby blanket and hugged it close to her heart. Betty held her hand and squeezed tight.

My mother and Betty, with all their fierce individual ambition, were nothing but fish carried by a great political tide. In the fragmented and tumultuous years after the Sino-Japanese War and before the People's Revolution, immigration from Shanghai to Hong Kong escalated steadily, until there were almost a million and a half new Shanghainese in the British territory. Small villages and towns all over China were taken over by the People's Liberation Army, and the major cities knew that they were next. Businessmen with patent leather shoes and briefcases vacated their offices. Many of the great Shanghai banks were closing down their main offices and relocating. Numerous artists, opera singers, engineers, dressmakers, poor laborers, and wealthy families alike all boarded the dilapidated train to Hong Kong, where the borders were miraculously open to refugees and the British government was fighting to keep the economy flush with capitalist funds.

The journey was arduous. My mother's train broke down twice, forcing the passengers to carry their belongings along the railway tracks until they reached the next platform, where they would wait, thirsty and exhausted, for a train that would allow them to enter the already jampacked cars. The rich passengers traveled in stylish luxury, breaking open bottles of champagne and instructing their servants to fetch water to wash in. The poor majority, like my mother, squeezed into stale and cramped compartments where they joked about the nonexistent toilets and tried to sleep sitting up.

When the two friends finally arrived in Hong Kong, they made their way from queue to queue, numb and exhausted. They registered as refugees and were dumped in a camp building with hundreds of other women, where they stayed for a few days while they regained their energy and talked to as many women as they could to figure out what their next move should be.

"There's a factory where they make plastic flowers, but the work is slow and you only get paid by the piece," said one woman.

"If I were you, I'd try the girlie bars in Wan Chai," said another. This area of Hong Kong was supposed to be a port of relaxation for sailors, marines, crewmen and businessmen. There was no lack for jobs there, all the women had heard. It was the nightlife playground of expats who had the means to dole out big tips. If you worked there, you'd get to wear makeup and fine cheongsams.

"Good money if you can get it," one older woman said, looking with a combination of envy and spite at my mother and Betty.

"It's the oldest profession, after all," another one said, giggling nastily.

The oldest profession? My mother, still a village girl at heart, didn't know what the older women meant at first. The understanding came to her later, while she was walking around the camp after dinner—she still liked to walk in the evenings—but she shrugged the idea off as cheap and unlikely. In her innocence, she thought that the job description sounded fantastic. She could wait tables and win over customers in her sleep. She had always admired fashion and tried her best to copy new styles with bargain fabric, so she particularly liked the idea of wearing silk dresses all day. Perhaps she would even get to perform as an actress, and become famous!

That night, as Betty packed their bags, my mother fell into a reverie, moving her hands gracefully through the air and humming the tune of a slow, romantic pop song. Betty looked at her with amusement and exasperation.

"What?" said my mother sheepishly.

"Do you know what a waitress at a girlie bar really does? Besides get the sailors to buy a drink?"

My mother drew her breath in. "I don't think that's true. I think it's just some of the girls. We don't have to."

"Just be careful never to borrow money from a stranger," Betty said, "You never know what they will demand for repayment. I heard they even hurt your family!" My mother cringed to think that she would ever be so desperate to get herself into such a situation. She was horrified to think that someone would look for Bobby and hurt him.

"No, no," my mother interrupted her own thoughts. "Stop spooking yourself!"

With their little bags clutched tight, they took a bus packed with people to Wan Chai, arriving at sunset, just as the streets were coming alive with street hawkers and strolling couples and neon lights.

As they asked multiple strangers which places were hiring, Betty and my mother were told over and over to look for a place called *Diamond Bar*. Outside the door, my mother was greeted by a rough sailor who was drunk and flirtatious. She had a bad feeling and told Betty she wasn't going in, and waited outside while Betty strode into the joint, determined to get a job. She watched as girls came out, hanging on to the arms of half-drunken men. They were laughing gaily, but my mother looked into the eyes of one of the women and knew she was faking the wildness that she gave off like the smell of cigarette smoke.

"Drink with a Hong Kong Doll," the sign at the door of the Diamond Bar said, with a sloppy addendum at the bottom: Most beautiful girls in town. My mother sighed sadly, leaning against the wall and gazing down at the rest of the street.

There was a sign in the wall of another place, a place that looked more like a cafe than a bar. She walked down the street and peeped through the front door. The place was called Imperial, and there were tables where people could order food and drinks, as well as a parquet circle in the middle of the room for couples who wanted to dance to old classics. There were beautiful girls in cheongsams sitting and talking politely to well-dressed businessmen. It was nothing like the scene at the girlie bar. She saw a sign that read, Help Needed. So she went up to the manager and asked if he wanted to hire a waitress.

"No," he said.

"Well, what is the help wanted sign for?"

"Hostesses. Must make conversation with the guests."

"What kind of conversation?" my mother asked.

"Interesting conversation."

My mother remembered James, and the long hours when they'd laughed together, translating jokes between English and Chinese. She decided to turn on her charm, smiled sweetly, and said, "I can make interesting conversation. But are we really talking about conversation, or something else?"

The manager said, decidedly indifferent, "Up to the girls."

My mother laughed. "How generous of you to allow them that choice!"

The two of them started talking. The manager thawed, taking a liking to my mother's bubbly personality, especially after she started speaking to him in comfortable, slangy English. After ten minutes, he hired her.

When Betty came out of the girlie bar, she'd gotten a job, and was astounded to see that my mother had gotten one as well—and one that involved nothing compromising, to boot. "There's always fine print," she said cynically. "No one tells you about the real stuff until you're in the door."

My mother shrugged. "There's no way to find out except to try!"

And if she hadn't tried, she wouldn't have met my father, she wouldn't have reluctantly fallen in love again, and I wouldn't be writing you this book today.

My father was born in a small town in Indonesia to a poor, ethnically Chinese couple who owned a store. He was smart and hard-working, and he learned Indonesian, Dutch, and English by the time he was a young teenager. Like my mother, he left his hometown at an early age to seek the opportunities of a bigger city. Renting one of three cots in a room that he shared with two other ambitious young men who had left their hometowns, he took on a series of menial jobs in Jakarta and kept his eyes peeled for bigger opportunities where new doors would open.

One day, he saw an advertisement for Dutch-speaking interns at a shipping company where he'd be able to sail the world on enormous ships. He applied for the job, waving aside his family's disbelief that he'd ever get it. And then, to everyone's surprise, he was offered the position. He received a uniform, splurged on a pair of new shoes, and showed up at the ship the day it was scheduled to sail. He was but five feet six inches tall with muscular arms from his solitary weightlifting—but he walked as if he was twice his size.

"Reporting for duty," he said with a smile, speaking with the carefully studied accent of a Dutch-Indonesian aristocrat.

It turned out that he loved sailing and took to it as naturally as if he had been born on a boat. In the middle of the ocean, in the pitch black of the night, he stared at the thousands of stars above him. He felt the shivering reaches of possibility, of untold wealth, of happiness. Who would have imagined that this boy from a small town would be on a major cargo ship serving with the Dutch officers? He pinched himself, but the stars remained, and so did his dreams. By the time he met my mother, he was a senior crewman, in charge of preparing payroll documents for all the crew on the ship.

One night, his ship docked in Wan Chai after a hard day of bad weather and rough waters.

"Imperial?" asked one of his friends. The other men nodded, familiar with the relaxed atmosphere and pretty women at the cafe. They washed their faces and hands, took shots of the cheap rice liquor that they kept stocked on the ship, and walked eagerly down the streets of Wan Chai, my father lagging behind.

My father had been to this cafe many times before. But unlike the majority of his shipmates, he wasn't in the practice of paying the women a little extra for special favors. Sentimental at heart, he craved nothing so much as domesticity, and the one downside of the life at sea was that it left him with no opportunities to really get to know women.

Still, some nights the air was warmly embracing and the atmosphere seemed full of potential. This was one of those nights. He smiled, feeling his spirits lift, and suddenly he stopped as the group approached the brightly lit Imperial Café. From the dark, rowdy street outside, he'd caught a glimpse of my mother standing at the hostess station, dressed in a tight brocade cheongsam with bright blue buttons at the neck. She was poised, slim, a few inches shorter than he was. Her jet-black hair was twisted in the back with a pearl pin. My father thought she was the most beautiful woman he had ever seen.

Inside Imperial, my mother was feeling none of the same magic. She leaned against the flimsy wooden podium and felt a familiar, uncomfortable malaise sink deep into her bones. She looked around the room, where her friends were either scheming to make more money from the sailors or vacantly seducing them.

She tried to push her gloom aside by making up stories. *There was once a princess who was trapped in a dungeon,* she thought. *She wrote love songs on her magical harp, and they were beautiful.* My father's shipmates walked in the door and my mother sighed. Then one day *the harp* broke and she had to talk to a group of boring sailors who walked into *the dungeon* and asked to be seated and ordered some nice cold beer. Grudgingly, she dissolved her reverie and got ready to feign interest in these customers.

My mother had a way of walking that made her appear as if she floated above the ground. My father noticed this immediately. As she made a joke about the day's bad weather, he memorized the sound of her easy, natural laugh. When the men took a seat in a booth, my father couldn't stop looking back at the hostess area as my mother stood there, beautiful and poised. He got up to go to the bathroom and stopped by the back station, where the manager sat over a pile of receipts. He asked the manager about the beautiful hostess. "Oh, that one. She just works here," the man said. "She doesn't leave the cafe with any men. So she's great for conversation, but that's about it."

Little did the manager know that his answer was exactly what my father longed to hear. He asked my mother to come keep him company, and spent the rest of the evening conversing with her at his table.

My mother made much less money than most girls who worked in Wan Chai, but she never questioned her life of abstention. She still lived with Betty, who was growing resentful and bitter towards the men who paid her for favors, and she saw the girlie bar life taking its toll on all the young women who worked there. Clinging to the consolation that they could send money home, and that they worked for themselves rather than for a pimp, the women were nevertheless stuck in a situation that frequently sapped their dignity and left them feeling like objects—and cheap ones, at that.

Every evening, my mother went home alone. Her boundaries were strictly defined; in her mind, she was still married to James. She hated going out, actually, especially with men who told her she was beautiful without ever really looking at her. She hated the way that every bit of conversation seemed to drive towards one meaningless end. "Want to get out of this place?" they would ask her, leering suggestively. Her answer was always, "Not tonight, sailor." She had mastered the art of quickly floating away from a man who got too close.

At the Imperial, she developed the reputation of being elusive and a little bit strange. Every night she went home just as the girls were heading out in a big group, and she'd put on the radio and dance with herself all night. She sang songs and read newspapers and reminded herself to be grateful for the chance to make money without compromising herself in any way. She wondered if her father had finally found a job back in Shanghai. Every day there was news of the People's

Revolution encroaching on the city, and she was worried that the borders would close before she could get Bobby out.

In the weeks after my father's first visit, she began to notice that the curiously polite sailor kept returning to see her.

Other people at the Imperial noticed too. "Staring at our beloved hostess again, I see," said the manager, who my father now knew well enough to call Bossman. He laughed.

"You're not the first one! Good luck with it."

"What do you mean?" asked my father.

"She's not going to put out for you," interjected another woman bluntly, "You're wasting your time. You know, she's quite the odd bird. She never goes out with us after work, and how about that!"

My father looked even closer at my mother, whose face looked sweet and contemplative as she thought about her son far away. He was sure he had fallen in love.

Over the next six months, my mother slowly warmed to my father's overtures. My father came to see her at Imperial every time he could find an excuse to be in Wan Chai. After finding out about her love for pretty fragrances, he bought her a bottle of Chanel No. 5 perfume. One night he asked her to dinner at the Ritz-Carlton, which struck her as terribly romantic and glamorous: an ideal occasion upon which to wear her Chanel No. 5.

Even after the Ritz—an evening when my mother felt like she was floating on a cloud of unexpected riches—it took her many months to drop the protective guardedness that she'd built around herself. It took her even longer to forget about James. But eventually she grew to love my father's intense focus on work, his realist's grasp on the post-war business world, and most of all his yearning to settle down and build a life of security and stability.

"I can take care of you," he told her over and over again. "Everyone can see that you're different from the other girls in here. You can't stay here forever or you'll miss out on life."

My mother went through her life with a theology built on superstition and childlike trust. When my father began to talk about marriage, she wondered if this was God's way of providing for her the same way He did when James walked into her life. Should she marry this man? She consulted a priest, who told her to pick the path of greater holiness.

Greater holiness? She wasn't sure what that meant. So she burned a candle and put two pieces of paper in a tin can: one reading *yes,* one reading *no.* When she shook the can, a piece of paper floated out and fell to the ground.

"Yes," she read. She took this as a divine sign that she should accept my father's proposal, and so she did.

Without fanfare, and with the pragmatic need to minimize costs, the two of them married at a government office on a day when my father was scheduled to set sail at five in the afternoon. As they said their vows, both he and my mother thought sadly about how he would be gone for the next five months. They spent every minute together right until the boat was ready to leave the dock. My mother walked her new husband to the port at sunset, as the boats lapped quietly against the grey water. Now that the moment of goodbye was imminent, she realized how much she didn't want to let him go. Instead of saying goodbye, she allowed him to kiss her, a kiss that lasted for minutes and seemed to stretch into hours, as strangers whistled.

Because of the speed of their courtship and my father's five-month stretches at sea, my mother did not make any plans to move out of the apartment she shared with Betty. When she arrived home in the twilight of her wedding day, Betty was padding around the kitchen in a robe, looking slightly green in the face.

"Are you okay?" asked my mother.

"So your businessman lover is finally gone," said Betty, giggling weakly.

My mother rolled her eyes but laughed along with her friend. "Yeah. Guess what? I married him."

"Good for you!" said Betty not knowing whether to take my mother seriously. She knew her friend was prone to seizing opportunities, though. *People like us don't have the luxury of hesitation,* my mother was fond of saying. "Well, now that you've got a man with some money, you can send more cash to your little genius in Shanghai." Abruptly, Betty ran to the bathroom and threw up.

My mother followed her, concerned. When Betty finally raised her head and rinsed out her mouth with water, there were tears in her eyes. My mother felt as if something terrible was about to happen.

"Did you really marry him?" Betty croaked out, head bent above the sink.

My mother laughed sadly and nervously. "Yes."

"Don't get knocked up," groaned Betty.

My mother's heart sank. "Oh no. Are you— you're not—"

Betty nodded, starting to shiver. "Unfortunately, I think I just might be."

Betty later learned it was exactly as she had feared. She was pregnant.

My mother had never seen Betty fall apart before. Her friend became like a crazy person, sending letter after letter to the man she was convinced had put her in this situation. He was a businessman with a family in the nicer part of Hong Kong, who came to the dance hall every now and then to buy Betty a few drinks and then disappear with her for an hour or two.

"He was going to leave his wife," wept Betty. "He told me he loved me and that he'd never met anyone like me."

These things that men say, thought my mother, *are nothing but lies.* She stroked her friend's hair. "It's going to be fine. Your baby and Bobby are going to be great friends, okay? We've made it this far. This isn't the end of everything. Let me make you some tea and we can talk about what your options are."

"My *options?*" shrieked Betty.

"Maybe we can travel back to Shanghai and you can stay there while you're pregnant, right? And then you can come back here with the baby. We'll make it somehow. I'll teach you how to sew, and we can open a dress shop or something." Even as she uttered these words she knew how unreal they were. There was no chance that Betty would ever be accepted by her family in China. She would shame the family. And there was nowhere to hide this shame.

"I'm getting rid of it," Betty said, hissing through her tears. "You are *joking* to think that I can take care of this baby. I came here with nothing, I still have nothing, and now I'm just another whore at the girlie bar. Not exactly mother material!" She started laughing hysterically, then crying again.

"Don't ever say that again," said my mother forcefully. She hugged her friend tight. They were silent for a long time. My mother finally spoke up. "I'll do whatever I can to help you, but at the very least you need to take a few days and think about this. And don't let me catch you calling yourself names. There are too many people in this world who are all too ready to do that for us."

Betty never changed her mind about the abortion. Against her wishes, my mother succumbed to the pressure from her friend. "Go with me or I go alone," said Betty. "Either way, I'm still going!" That was how it happened that my mother stuffed her wallet with cash, covered Betty's face and shoulders with an old pink shawl, and brought her to an anonymous, grease-streaked, trash-ridden alley in Wan Chai. There, a small door opened and the two of them went downstairs and a well-meaning quack doctor with a filthy coat hanger performed the act that none of them wanted to be witnessing. Betty, unevenly numb and sedated from the amateur anesthetic, screamed voicelessly. My mother held herself in, trying not to think about Bobby, wondering at the sheer ugliness and desperation and danger of being a woman sometimes. It was such a gift, to be able to give someone life—but in Betty's case, she saw a child as her biggest curse.

Betty was never the same after that day. She was sick for weeks, depressed for months. When my father came back from his five-month voyage at sea, he found my mother morose at the cafe, thinking about her friend, who had just gotten fired and had found work at a seedier, more decrepit

Choices at the Crossroads

place. Even her happiness at seeing my father was tempered with the melancholy of knowing that someone she loved was beyond her help.

As my parents made plans for the future, my mother couldn't stop worrying about what would happen once she moved out of the apartment she still shared with Betty. "What is she going to do without me?" she cried to my father late one night. Betty's heart was absolutely broken by the man she had been wrong to trust, broken by the black-market doctor and the idea of the child she chose not to bring into this world.

My father mistrusted Betty and felt wildly possessive of my mother, whom he had forced to stop working at the cafe immediately after he returned from his voyage. "You're not her mother," he said flatly. "Stop worrying about it. You would do well to never see Betty again."

When my mother lugged the last box out of the apartment, Betty was composed and seemingly nonchalant. "Well, at least one of us made it out of this place," she said with a slight grin.

Six months later, my mother ran into a mutual friend who knew her and Betty. "Did you hear?" the friend asked.

"Did I hear what?" my mother answered.

"Betty killed herself," her friend said, robotically, as if she were reporting the evening news. "Yeah, yeah, so sad. She overdosed on pills."

My mother didn't say a word. She walked back to the apartment with her mind racing. She realized that she had lost Betty the day she moved out. Did Betty know it killed her to walk away? Was she wrong to always be hiding her deepest emotions? Could she have shown Betty how much it had all meant to her—starting with the first day that Betty had taken a walk with her and Bobby throughout the broken, war-torn city of Shanghai?

My mother was used to living life in circumstances where she had no choices, where she had to make all her decisions coldly and without sentiment. Sentiment was another luxury, like hesitation, and my mother had no time for it. Still, in the months since she had moved out of the apartment, my mother hid a secret hope that one day Betty would show up at her doorstep with her crooked smile, a joke, a word of encouragement, and love.

How foolish, she thought to herself. With Betty's death, their separation was permanent. She had lost her best friend forever. And, as she suspected, she would never have a friend like that again.

Why does God protect us from some events and not from others? I used to obsess over this question. God did not protect my mother against the man who raped her. But God protected her in the cafe, allowing her to make a living without selling herself. God also protected me while I was growing up in a three-floor building, with a bar on the first level and a brothel on the third. Yet, He seemed to have abandoned all protection when it came to my mother's suicide. Why did He allow her to go through so much? Why did He allow me to see the sight of my mother's body, limp and lifeless in the middle of our family's living room?

Over time, I've tried to let this question go and remember that through it all, God has a plan. He always intends suffering to have a purpose. He was not afraid to let His own Son be crucified on a cross because of the power of that sacrifice to pay the penalty of sin.

My mother always loved and clung to this aspect of God, because she knew all that it meant to give up a son. In her final mental breakdown, she thought of the power of God's sacrifice without ever confronting the fruitlessness of her own.

Now, long after my mother's act almost destroyed my family, I marvel that God was able to make her sacrifice bear fruit. He has transformed my family's loss into my passion for women's ministry. Through Inspire Women, I continue to meet women who have witnessed God transform suffering into healing—who have made it through circumstances that would have been enough to crush them, had they not trusted in God.

Let me give you an example. One young woman named Lisa came to the ministry requesting a scholarship to continue with her studies. She told us that she had a strong passion to work with at-risk youth, and without batting an eyelash, she stated, "I definitely understand where troubled teenagers are coming from. My step-father sexually molested me continuously. I could not stand it anymore and ran away when I was 16 and lived under a bridge." As I listened to her story, I could hear echoes of my own mother in Lisa's voice. Like Lisa, my mother had been trapped in a situation she could not change. She did her best to overcome what had happened to her. At her first chance of escape, she bolted out the door and kept running. She never looked back until one day she saw the opportunity to put her suffering behind her. She married James as her way to find a new life, and when that life failed, she had the courage to dream again, marrying my father in the magistrate's offices in Hong Kong. She, like Lisa, understood the priceless gift of a person who comes into your life and gives you a second, third, or even fourth chance to start over.

As it often happens with women who have seen too much, Lisa's suffering gave her a deep understanding and empathy for those who live on the dark side of life. Because she had been entrapped by her step-father, she understood what abuse did to the human soul. She had the experience of walking into a church and letting the presence of God wash her white as snow. She walked out feeling like she had been given a clean slate. She was inspired to use her life to reach back into the darkness to help those who were still in bondage.

In her appeal for help, she said, *If you don't help me, then all I have left are my memories. Please give meaning to my suffering and help me change suffering into purpose.*

It has always been my mission that Inspire Women would function like the friend God always wanted us to have. A friend with the anchor of God's Word and the faith to live according to its teachings. A friend who is God in the flesh, offering clarity in the confusion, believing in God's power of restoration when dreams die.

Although my mother and Betty were best friends, they lacked a strong spiritual framework and a larger community. They became unmoored from each other and then, finally, from themselves. If only Betty had believed in her own self-worth and her right to be respected! If only my mother had known how vital her best friend would be in her own emotional survival! If they had trusted God and stayed by each other's sides, they might have been able to keep the music of hope from fading into deadly silence. Today they might still be on earth, still dreaming and realizing those dreams.

These two women, and their similar tragic ends, are just one example of the fact that spiritual isolation can wreck your soul. I've always felt so upset that this lonely condition can occur even at the heart of many Christian communities. It took me many years of searching to find a community of people who refused to judge another's past, present, or future. It was even harder to find a group of individuals who were ready not just to pray but to move their feet—to act on and invest in the potential of their friends and fellow Christians.

I have learned that a cross on the door is no guarantee of holiness. I learned this lesson for the first time in elementary school, at a Christian school. I saw a second-grade girl in the playground with the soles of her shoes nearly falling off. The stitches, ragged and worn, were on the brink of unraveling.

The other kids thought it was funny. They pushed her around and stepped on her feet, screeching with laughter. By the end of the day, the girl was walking completely flat-footed, dragging her shoes from place to place in order for the soles not to fall off.

I felt sure when a teacher saw this, she would immediately step in to stop the bullying. Maybe one of them would help her with glue or thread to get her through the day. Yet one particular spiritual leader openly ridiculed the girl when she saw the sorry state of her feet.

"Can't your parents afford shoes?" she said sharply. "This is a respectable school and you need to look respectable."

I was young when this happened, but I remember understanding for the first time how deeply divisive and harmful it is to judge yourself as better than others and to destroy someone's self-worth for the sake of your "respected institution." As my mother said to Betty, there are enough people out there who are quick to come to superficial conclusions; shouldn't those who say they represent God's message be the first to acknowledge the fact that we are all imperfect people needing each other's support?

My mother understood the games people played to win acceptance. She knew the human tendency to cast out anyone different or down on their luck. She experienced the judgment of society harshly, starting at age 14, when she realized that even her family would somehow blame her for being raped. Later on, she never looked down on Betty or the other girls for their compromising work at the girlie bar. Further on in life, in our family's small apartment where faint, disturbing screams floated down the hallways from the brothel upstairs, I think she felt a deep sympathy for the prostitutes who were stuck in that world.

Once I saw a girl from upstairs crying on the steps outside our apartment. It seemed that a john had hit her, and her face was swollen, purple and bleeding. I felt so terrible for her. I went inside my door and told my mom, asking her, "Why? Why do these ladies live like this? Why don't they go out and do something else?"

"Maybe they can't," my mother said. "If they try to leave, maybe they will be killed. Don't ever make the mistake of thinking that they're content with the way people see them. They hate being seen as trash. But they're stuck, and there's nothing they can do."

Just as my mother taught me not to judge the down-trodden, she told me to never make judgments about the wealthy. "It's easy to assume that someone's life is perfect," she told me. "But the people you envy may be drowning in secret tears."

This, maybe, is the secret to authentic friendship and community: we should see people not for the roles they play in society but for the hearts they have and the potential they bear.

Think of Betty. My mother saw her friend as a fellow woman, refusing to define her by the roles that she did and did not fulfill. To do so would have been pointless. Betty sold her body. Did that make her first a prostitute? She sacrificed her dignity to send money to her family and support her sick grandmother. Did that make her first a daughter, or a granddaughter? She became pregnant. If she had the baby, would that make her first a mother?

Betty, like my mother, felt the shame and obligation of these competing roles every day. I wish that they could have understood that they were first and foremost simply women, made by God, daughters of the King.

We yearn so much for clarity, for everything to be either black or white. My mother's story shows me that life often unfolds in the grey. And in these grey areas I see the need to have boundaries. Some people see boundaries as restrictive—but my mother's story has taught me that perhaps these internal or spiritual boundaries are designed to serve as fences to keep us from falling over a cliff.

Of course, at the end of the day, as hard as we try, we will always fall short of perfection. The longer I live, the more I can see that the best intentions have never prevented me, my mother, or anyone else from making a lot of mistakes. I need a Savior to make right all my wrong choices. And I need friends who will stand by me and embody this Savior every day.

CHAPTER 4

Clarity through Flashbacks

Stand with me for a minute at the entrance to the three-floor apartment building in which I spent my early childhood years. To the right of the door that I hesitate to enter is a bar, its windows flashing boldly with neon lights. To the left is a restaurant, with a huge display of steamed dumplings in neat rows. If you were to enter this building, you would see a straight flight of concrete steps leading upwards. In the open space behind the staircase, a hawker, his wife, his toddler, and infant have created a makeshift home. At the top of the stairs is a brothel, where the noise from the rented bedrooms seeps into our walls. On the middle floor is the apartment that I shared with my parents and sister, where I huddled for five-hour stretches over self-assigned homework while my parents snapped viciously at each other over the prices of fruit and fish.

And outside this building, the clacking of British boots and the sound of shattering glass; the muffled roar of a mob tearing through the streets in the distance; the threat and the presence of riots getting closer and closer each night. Grey smoke floats above our neighborhood, full of women too rushed for conversation, street vendors hollering their wares and men sitting in alleys between buildings, puffing a cigarette or losing their minds in the game of mahjong. My mother inhales the newspaper and exhales paranoia. I am afraid of all lone objects—are they bombs?—on the street.

I am eleven years old. Through shrewd flattery, our good test scores, and her excellent tea eggs, my mother has coaxed a mission school run by Italian nuns to push me and my sister up on the waiting list. ("So strict," she cried happily to my father, "and for just $12 a month!") My sister and I leave our apartment in our snow-white uniforms every morning and return every afternoon, occasionally averting our eyes from incidents we know our mother wouldn't want us to see.

We know the rules; we have to ring the doorbell at the bottom of the stairs before we enter the building. When our mother hears the bell, she opens the door and peers down the stairway, making sure that there are no assailants lying in wait. If the stairway is empty, she calls down to us, and we run up the stairs as fast as possible, our school bags rattling against our backs. She hugs us, always so relieved to see us safely back home.

Through the window, we hear the thunderous footfalls of another politically incited riot. My mother calmly makes us a snack. I start on my homework while my mother pretends that life is normal, even though tear gas is filling the street. Welcome to Hong Kong in the 1960's.

This was almost a decade after my parents first met, and a sea of change had long ago occurred in the relationship between them. My mother was no longer that buoyant, graceful hostess from Wan Chai, and my father was no longer a love-struck sailor with stars in his eyes. Even in my earliest memories, the two of them were already molded completely by their obligations to me and my sister. My mother's identity was that of a mother—a housewife, a worrier, a coach, a teacher—and my father was a provider, thinking only of salaries and survival.

Their whirlwind romance struggled, as so many do, with the onslaught of money troubles that came with settling down. My father's new desk position with the Dutch shipping company paid less than his previous career at sea, and it didn't take long after they moved into a new apartment for him to see that it would be a struggle to keep up with the expenses of marriage and children.

The best plans made by human minds often don't line up with what transpires next, especially when it comes to pregnancy. After my sister Rosita was born, my parents were not ready financially for another child. However, a year later, my mother found herself balancing my sister on her hip as she vomited into the toilet. All day she waited for my father to come home from work, trembling with anxiety. When he walked in the door, she blurted it out: "I think I'm pregnant again."

My father dropped his briefcase. The two of them stared at each other, trying to quench the dread that both of them felt rising in their throats. My mother, trying to be optimistic, said, "Maybe we'll have a son. That will be perfect. We'll together have one boy and one girl." For the following months, my mother prayed for this small consolation, that this unwanted child would at least be a boy.

With that sort of welcome into the world, of course I spent most of my young life wishing that I could just get out of everyone's way! Meanwhile, my parents loved intensely and also fought intensely. Through their fights, it didn't take me long to pick up the additional fact that the family hadn't been ready for me, and if there had to be an unwanted pregnancy, it would have been so much better to have been a boy.

Is this a lot for a young child to know? I should explain that my mother told me everything—maybe too much. She and I were each other's best friends, starting when I was too young to understand the sadness that occasionally overtook her. Sometimes I think that I was around 8 years old when I grew up completely. I remember that was the year when I noticed that the fighting in my house was abnormal, when I understood what my mother meant when she told me I had been an accident, and when I realized that there was a real possibility that she would hurt herself.

By the time my sister and I were adolescents, these fights between my mother and my father escalated into screaming matches that always ended the same way. "Why don't *you* try to pay for all this stuff!" my father would shout at her. "Oh, that's right—you have no education and no way of earning money! Now, what was it you wanted again?" This insult worked every time, making my mother newly ashamed of her impoverished background, forcing her to her bedroom where she would cry in silence while I sat beside her, holding her hand.

"You'd be better off without me," she'd sob.

"That's not true at all," I'd tell her.

"I'm no use. At least your father can provide for you. And this way you won't have to endure all this fighting all the time. It's no way to grow up." The desperation in her voice was palpable.

In times like this, I would grow fearful. I made her promise that she would never leave me, and when the fog of sadness lifted, she would become a mother again, reassuring me that she would never walk out or commit suicide. "My best friend did that. I'd never do that. She left behind so much pain, and I'd never do that to you." Sometimes, unexpectedly, she would cheer up completely. "Don't be silly! How could I leave you, my baby?" she'd say to me with a note of happiness in her voice.

Always, I could see that part of what sustained my mother was the possibility—no matter my father's protests—of going to America. "Things will be different in America," she would murmur, repeating this to me over and over. The word *America* itself developed an instant connotation of free land, big spaces, and dreams come true. When she talked about America, the suffocation we felt in our little apartment would begin to lift. From a very young age, I decided to make this dream my own. So I said to her, "Don't worry. Just give me time. Everything's going to be okay, Mama."

But of course I was a child and I couldn't grow up fast enough to keep the ground from crumbling under my mother's feet. I could not rescue her when she could no longer hold on, when U.S. Immigration denied her petition and shut down her deepest wishes. She blamed my father, accusing him of not showing enough enthusiasm during the interview at the U.S. Immigration office. *Who can you trust to protect your dreams?* I wondered.

I saw, as a child, that a woman's dream is the last to receive attention when discretionary income is low. My mother had too many limitations to be able to afford her earnest hopes, and no one else was around to tell her that she deserved to have them.

Eventually, she herself accepted this position, becoming a willing part of the family idea that she existed just to support the rest of us. In my early childhood, I used to see her studying around the house, preparing to earn her long-belated high school diploma. But at some point, she chose to dedicate all her energy to my sister's and my schoolwork. Like many mothers, she chose to be selfless: if it came down to helping herself or helping her children, she'd choose the children every time. I don't recall if she ever graduated. If she did, there was no fanfare or celebration. The greater likelihood is that she didn't finish school or if she did, decided that the little education she was able to get did not make any difference and she could not justify taking more of the family's discretionary income for herself. One day, all her books that were sprawled out on the table just vanished and I never saw them again. I didn't know then that with the disappearance of the books something inside her also died.

I was young when my education about different social classes began, on the weekends that I'd spend tagging along with my father on his trips to the country club, where he played tennis every Saturday and Sunday.

This country club was the one luxury that my parents made room for, no matter if it meant that we had to forgo meat and skimp on rice. My father was insistent that he deserved this outlet from work, and my mother readily agreed, knowing that it would benefit me to see a world outside my ramshackle, vice-ridden neighborhood. Most of the club members were British, and their children were quite different from the kids I knew at school.

Yet in my innocence, I had no idea that I was from a vastly different socioeconomic class than these children. I didn't even know if *they* noticed this; my father was terrific at communicating in high circles, and my mother still retained her skill of making designer-looking clothing out of bargain fabrics from the market. It never occurred to me that we never invited any of our club friends back to our home—or that doing so would make both my parents feel very ashamed.

Those weekends at the country club were full of contrasts, going from the prim and proper country club and the frenzies of our neighborhood. I was a shy and observant child, and I watched our neighbors silently. At night I watched the exhausted kitchen boys who worked at the restaurant, as they slumped into the small room with its crowded bunk beds, ready to pass out in the company of a dozen other exhausted workers. I watched the tailor who lived across from them work at his table—he was always toiling, even though he seemed ancient—cutting fabric all day and night.

I saw their lives and I witnessed their pain; I watched, helpless, as the pain crept closer. First, my girlfriend in the neighborhood was raped while coming back from school. And then, just a few months later, I was working quietly at the kitchen table when I heard my mother yelling, running up the stairs with heavier footsteps following her. She screamed for me to open the door. I was frozen by panic for an instant, then pulled the door open just enough for my mother's frantic body to push through. I saw a pair of hands grabbing for her. I slammed the door, just barely missing the man's fingertips.

My mother's repeated message during my childhood years still resonates in my ears—that life was hard, and there was no use judging anyone. Some people were lucky enough to be born into comfort, some people were not, and everyone deserved compassion, consideration, and respect.

One year, a work friend of someone in the country club moved to Hong Kong. Somehow, my mother became involved in helping the wife get settled in our city. They became part of my family's life, and I came to know them as our great friends, Mr. and Mrs. Tang.

It didn't take long before I realized that this family was not like mine at all. First, their living space was ten times bigger than ours, and they had maids and chauffeurs aplenty. But what really got me to see their wealth was one tubful of lychees, an abundance that spoke to me of luxury more than diamonds ever could.

I loved lychees, and so did my mother. When the sweet fruit was in season, she rejoiced when we had enough money to purchase a dozen to share among our four-person household. But Mrs. Tang bought lychees like they were grains of rice. While at their house, I saw one enormous wooden bucket full to bursting with the brown fruit, lying around as if it meant nothing.

"Wow," I said to myself. "This is what being rich must be like."

Through Mrs. Tang, I was exposed to the extravagant everyday lifestyle of the wealthy. Parties took on a dimension beyond anything I had ever seen, and I remember one wedding in particular with a guest list of thousands of people. Parents had a personal chauffeur and another for the children. Money solved every problem; if things got bad, you could always send for a minister who would come to your home, who would pray for your blessing in exchange for a check.

But the longer I knew this family, the more I saw the facade break down. Once, I saw Mrs. Tang wailing, prostrate on the floor, with her hands wrapped around her husband's ankles. I don't think they knew I was upstairs in the house, playing with their children, and I glimpsed them from an open balcony as they physically fought each other.

Later, I found out why: Mr. Tang had been involved with someone else's wife for years. He then persuaded his wife to commit adultery to mitigate his own guilt. These affairs had been going on behind the scenes for a long time, and when Mrs. Tang told her husband to stop, he was outraged and refused to listen to her. In pathetic protest, she began to resort to tactics like this—clinging to his ankles in order to physically prevent him from leaving the house.

That day, he coldly kicked her loose and ignored her wailing and pleading. He didn't have time for theatrics, he said; he had to go and close a deal that would generate millions of dollars. He had all the financial power and as far as he was concerned, he ruled the world.

It was the same power dynamic that my parents dealt with that so many women still deal with today. Whether in the poorest of neighborhoods or in the wealthiest ones, it's always the same: when you are desperate for love from someone who feels they have all the financial power, you say goodbye to your dignity. Sometimes when you say goodbye too often, you kill your own soul and exist as an outer shell of your real self, with no emotions left.

I don't know what happened with Mr. and Mrs. Tang. They moved out of our lives when their business relocated them. And just like that, the purpose for them in my life was over. Later, when I started my work with Inspire Women, I felt incredibly grateful that I had grown up with feet planted both in the world of the poor and the world of the affluent. I marveled at a God who was in control from the very beginning. He had a plan for my life and my mother was preparing me for it. Part of that plan included working with the wealthy.

At the mission school, I became part of a group of girlfriends whose parents were all counting on us to find a way out. Finding a scholarship to an American university was our collective obsession, and we talked about it endlessly without ever really knowing how we could achieve it aside from working as hard as we could. Our research began when we were fifteen. We wrote to college after college, and any time someone had a new lead, we would all jump at the opportunity. We didn't have the luxury to weigh our options, because we barely had access to any. Back then, any open door gave us a glimpse of light.

We were ecstatic when we started actually succeeding in our goal of getting out. When it was time for me to leave, I was sure that all talk about keeping in touch was just small talk to feel better. In reality, I understood that each person would be facing new challenges in a new country, and that she would be busy finding a way to rescue the rest of her family. There was nothing more we could do for each other but to wish each other well.

Is this terribly unsentimental? Letting people go was something I learned from my mother, who had always lived a life where she had to leave people behind. It wasn't because we wanted to lose our friends—we simply had to do so, and we coped as best we could by just getting on with life. I tried to apply this logic to the situation after my mother committed suicide.

But perhaps this wasn't healthy after all. I was doing some research recently on "ambiguous loss." The research spoke of the hidden losses that people hold onto for years, pressured by society into keeping up appearances while they are swallowed by helplessness inside.

The problem with ambiguous losses is simply that the person is never given permission to mourn properly. Grief piles upon grief until one day the person overflows with losses that were never validated.

Often, I've wondered if writing this book is a way to define all of my losses—and perhaps my mother's, too—and finally let them go.

When my mother left my brother in China, Bobby was only seven. Her intentions to send for him failed miserably when the Communist government shut the borders a year after my mother left China and assumed an isolationist policy. She did not see my brother again until he was seventeen.

By this time, our family was a little stronger financially, and my father agreed to allow my mother to try to find a way to get her son out of China. I'm not really sure how he got out, but when he arrived in Hong Kong I wasn't cognizant of who he was—I was only a toddler at the time.

I can't imagine how emotional this experience was for my mother, because as soon as my brother arrived in Hong Kong he decided to head for America. He threw himself into his studies and won a full scholarship. My mother secretly gave him six hundred dollars to float him in the States for a few months—money that she'd received by pawning pieces of jewelry she collected for a decade. She also gave him a diamond ring and said, "Sell this if you need money."

Later, when I found out the steps that he had taken to preserve the ring, and honor his mother's tribute, I wondered if the ring was the only item my brother possessed of hers. He still holds on to the ring today. To think he slept in a flophouse in New York City, barely eating, working his way up from the lowest jobs that a person could have and never sold that ring. And he reached senior Vice President at a Fortune 500 company without selling that ring. Just goes to show you that my mother was right: America was the land of opportunity for her children.

More than a decade after my brother left for New York, both my sister and I won full scholarships to American universities. We were both scheduled to leave in the summer of 1974. My sister was two years older than me and could have left earlier; however, she chose to wait until I graduated so we could leave the country together. She filled her time taking secretarial courses, frequently reminding me that I was the one delaying the adventure.

My sister talked tough, but her heart was tender towards me. She always tried to protect me. I know that her waiting for me to graduate so she could leave the country at the same time was one of the ways she was trying to protect her baby sister.

There was only one problem: my parents couldn't go. U.S. Immigration had denied my parents their visas. They didn't have the skills that America needed and Bobby had yet to receive citizenship which was required to sponsor them. As her daughters were making plans to leave, my mother felt she would be left behind for the rest of her life. My mother, who had spent her whole life trying to escape from one thing or another, began to feel the full impact of what she saw as a final failure. Overnight, she plunged into depression. She had been sad before, so I was convinced she would snap out of her blues. But her depression grew so deep that she couldn't dig herself out. And then the depression turned into a breakdown.

One night, in my last year of high school, I hunched over the kitchen table furiously working. I noticed my mother standing over me and ignored her. As I worked, her shadow kept hovering. She wouldn't go away.

"What do you want?" I yelled, like any petulant adolescent would.

"Tell me you'll be fine without me," she said softly. She'd said this so many times before that I was almost immune to the sentence's meaning.

"I'll be fine without you!" I cried carelessly. "Can I just do my work now?"

The next morning, I woke up and I realized she was trying to say goodbye. She just needed to know her baby would be fine.

I have spent years thinking about that final exchange between my mother and me. How could I not regret it? How could I possibly atone for such cruelty towards a woman who gave me everything? I should have been more sensitive to what she was saying. For the longest time, I told myself that I could have stopped her.

Now, I am beginning to let this guilt go. I try to be clear-headed and acknowledge that there was nothing I could do. People don't just go off and kill themselves because you say something thoughtless. The situation had been beyond help for a year and a half. She had grown fearful and paranoid, no longer afraid of rapists on the street but concerned with shadowy, imaginary boogeymen who were out to hurt her and her daughters. When I would ask her what was wrong, she would say, "They're watching us."

"Who?" my father and my sister would ask.

"Just you wait. They're watching us," she'd say. At the time, I read her fear as believing that some greater force was against her—a way of looking for the reason why her dream of America was falling through. Now I can see that she was truly melting down in her grief; her body could not take one more disappointment. Her eyes began to dart back and forth like a nervous animal. She cautioned us daily, sure that harm was around the corner. Sometimes, she spoke of someone tracking her down. Was this a true gap in her story from the past? I can never be sure. It was taboo to speak of mental illness in this society, and even after she died, we told everyone it was because of a heart attack.

I would be inclined to think that her fears were imagined, except for one memory. Once, when I came home from school, there was a man sitting in our living room who looked very official. My mother sounded like she was negotiating. Was she negotiating her life? Or was she negotiating our lives, or our citizenship? I'll never know. She rushed me to my room and told me not to come out. When the man left I emerged from hiding and asked, "Who was that?"

She said, "I told you. They've found us." This scared me so much that I never asked about it again.

As we packed up and tidied my mother's things in the wake of her suicide, I saw a book on her nightstand table. It was *The Imitation of Christ* by Thomas à Kempis. The book had been thumbed to pieces, its spine long ago broken.

Here and there, a phrase was highlighted. My eye fell on one in particular.

"There is no greater love than when a friend lays down his life for another," I read out loud to myself, all alone in the room where my mother used to live. All her life, her role had been to save her family. She had confused herself with the Savior who saved the world by sacrificing Himself. Did she think she was showing me *love?*

She hadn't saved anyone. And I certainly didn't feel like the recipient of love. I thought of the riots and the tear gas of my childhood. This was the final, most terrible bomb; my mother had detonated her own lost hopes and shattered my world into a thousand pieces.

Throughout my childhood, I felt like my mother's life and my life were one and the same. I was her greatest hope, her best friend, her confidante, and her sister. She couldn't have an independent life separate from me; I was always involved and charged with rescuing her life.

Before I stood any chance of reassembling my life, I had to first express the unfathomable despair that was swallowing me. I had to stop attempting to bring back my mother's presence, and I had to allow God to show me each being is accountable to Him.

I was not created to save my mother and only God could turn an irreversible loss into a new plan for my life.

CHAPTER 5

The Wilderness Years

After the funeral, my sister and I kept ourselves busy preparing to leave. To our surprise, our father encouraged us relentlessly, taking on the role that my mother had left vacant. We feared for his well-being—how could a man stand to lose his wife and two daughters within six months? But he cheered us on. "You've worked all your life for this moment," he told us. Many times, I wished my mother could have seen how my father supported her dream after she was gone. How, when he could have insisted that we stay, he gave us the courage to go.

I spent hours wondering what to pack for America. I could only bring two suitcases, and most importantly, as my father liked to remind me, I couldn't take my doll.

The doll had straight brown hair and a soft body, like a real baby. It was one of the few gifts that my parents

93

had given me in my early childhood, and so I had grown completely attached to it. My mother used to prop the doll up on my bed, lying on its belly with its legs crisscrossed behind its back, with one elbow down and the other hand holding up the doll's chin. I had come home every day seeing this doll waiting for me in my room, a symbol to me that life was in order—that everything would go on, at least for another day.

"That doll has no place in your new life," my father said firmly. And really, I agreed with him. But hadn't I already had to grow up too fast? Wasn't my mother committing suicide enough of a reason to take a silly toy that had always comforted me? "Absolutely not," he said.

I packed the doll away, deep in an old dresser, feeling like I was cutting my own umbilical cord.

I had another goodbye to say during these days—not to my doll, but to my boyfriend, a student at the University of Hong Kong. I'd met him at an organized dance, where my all-girls mission school partnered up with the students and alumni of a similar boys' school.

This boy was sweet and protective. He'd just returned from four years of college in America, and kept telling me that I was too innocent to face the challenges of that fast-paced and confusing country. He would always put the same song on his record player: "Oh baby, baby, it's a wild world." He'd sing along. He promised to write me every week.

My sister and I left for America together, in the shimmering heat of the summer of 1974. I had just turned eighteen and Rosita was one day short of turning twenty. As we navigated the airport together, I was reminded of when we would go to the market as children. My mother always said,

"Hold each other's hands. When I am no longer here, you'll have to remember that you have each other!"

So we held hands as we walked across the concourse, to the gate. It felt strange to be the passenger, to wave good-bye to my father. I looked at him, a small figure far away, and thought for the first time that he was not going to do well without me. I pictured him returning to a completely empty home. *Is it easier to die than to live and have to figure out how to make it without your loved ones?* I wondered. *Was this how my mother felt when she left Shanghai after losing her first husband?*

The passengers behind me pushed me through the plane doors and I went numbly to my seat, wondering what would become of me. As the pretty stewardess mimed putting on an oxygen mask, I put my arms around myself and squeezed. I imagined that these arms were the arms of my mother, the arms of God, the arms of someone who could give me the courage and confidence to enter my future. A deep exhaustion swept over me and, thankfully, I fell asleep for nearly the entire flight.

Many hours later, our plane began to descend over the nighttime panorama of New York City. This was America, and I was really here. I was filled with an instant euphoria at having finally fulfilled a dream that had begun in my mother's heart so many decades ago—and at the same time, I felt a familiar emptiness creep in underneath.

I was like an athlete who had trained for years in the Olympics; here I was, holding my gold medal, and my coach was not with me. This was the first moment that I experienced the strange duality that I would soon understand to be a common side effect of life in America: that you could be politically free, you could accomplish all the mini-goals of your dream, but still you could live in a bottomless emotional hell.

Who would guide me through my days here? Who would remind me to sing when I was too serious? I found myself going through my memory bank to piece together the time I had shared with my mother, so I could put together some kind of a script for the rest of my life. Then I stopped myself.

If I keep thinking of my life as her dream, I'll have nothing but fumes to keep me going, I told myself. *This is the point where the dream becomes mine, not hers. This is the point where I decide how this journey will go.*

Churning this idea over and over in my head, I fell into my brother's arms when he met my sister and me at the airport. There, I met my sister-in-law for the first time. She was a tall woman, nearly six feet tall, with gorgeous red hair. Their daughter was five years old, hiding behind her mother but trembling with nervous excitement. According to my brother, she'd been telling everyone at school that she had two aunts coming in all the way from Hong Kong.

All the women in the family were nervous, but my brother was his calm self. "You made it," he said. "Welcome to America." I noticed a smile in his eyes. He was more practiced at moving on with life than we were. I was holding off my sadness, thinking, "If only my mother could be here"—but Bobby was probably thinking, "Let's move on and get these girls some dinner." I dragged my two suitcases, and tried not to think about my doll or my boyfriend.

In the next few days, I asked my brother for advice about college. I was so excited about having the freedom to choose my course of study. I had a dozen competing inter-ests at once, and I figured I would just take any class that seemed interesting.

"Study business," my brother said, shaking his head at my frivolous unfocused approach. "You're here to make it, and you can't forget that. You're not an American kid. You need to major in whichever area will get you a job." He was only trying to protect me, but I almost felt angry. I hadn't even tried anything new yet! What happened to my idea of being a writer? My brother said, "Writers can't feed themselves unless they are the absolute best." Was he saying I could never be the best? Or was he saying I would starve before I got there, if I ever got there?

It felt like a door was slowly sliding closed, but I trusted my brother, who had already achieved so much success. When I registered for classes, I picked all the introductory economics and math classes I needed to complete a business major—then added on a psychology class and an English seminar, just for fun. *This is the free land of America,* I said defiantly in my head. *I can do whatever I want.*

My boyfriend and I had made an agreement that we would call each other every month for five minutes. It was a stupid, cost-saving idea, and it ended up being more pain-ful than it was good. Five minutes is an excruciatingly short amount of time to hear the voice of the person you love, and our phone call just made it difficult to concentrate on form-ing a new life without him.

A few weeks before my second semester ended at Mis-sissippi University for Women, I received an unexpected letter. *Dear Anita,* I read. *You are too emotional. I cannot concentrate on my studies in medical school. So I must end this relationship.*

You know how young love and heartbreak feels, don't you? Like a punch in the gut, over and over, until you can't think anymore. I was such a bottomless pit in those days; I was working so hard and holding on to such faraway hopes in a desperate attempt to cover up my despair. My boyfriend's horribly businesslike letter confirmed what I had suspected: that I was completely alone in this world.

I thought about all the things he had told me—that he would protect me, that he would wait for me forever—and felt so ashamed for trusting him. Hadn't I seen it well enough that dreams and loves and relationships don't last? Didn't I know that people sometimes simply had to leave the people they loved in order to move on and protect their own future?

Thankfully, I had befriended a freshman girl who had invited me to spend the summer with her. The time I spent with her distracted me from my anguish. She was a missionary's daughter. Her father was a doctor and her family had just relocated back to the United States after spending years building a church in Africa. I loved her family, and I was intrigued by their sincere desire to serve other people. Their life was not about protecting a career or achieving financial security for themselves; rather, they opened their home to foreign students who had nowhere to go and they spent years away from home. The serving of others was a side of America I had not seen

"Who *does* that?" I thought, more confused than anything.

Although their choices were noble, I had too much anxiety to consider giving my life away to service. I had to accumulate degrees and get a good job. I had to pay the bills and fulfill my commitment to my mother to be independent and never rely on a man again. Still, I think a seed was planted in me that summer: I saw how happy they were, investing in their communities and dedicating their lives to other people.

When school started again the next semester, I went into overdrive. I knew I needed to save money and be efficient, so I was determined to finish my four-year degree in two years. The dean had approved my petition to take a double course load of twenty-four credit hours —"You're the first person to ever ask me to take *more* classes," he said skeptically— fortunately, I was able to get some of the classes I took in Hong Kong accepted for credit. My roommate, who was also from Hong Kong, joined me in this relentless push for success. We pulled all-nighters on a regular basis and ran around from class to class like we were insane. It kept us from missing home, even if we weren't exactly well rested.

At the time, I was also trying to distract myself from the letters that my father kept sending me. With the death of my mother, without anyone to provide for, he seemed to have rediscovered his emotional side. *The loneliness is killing me,* he wrote. *Please come back as soon as you can.*

"One more year," I told myself. "Then you can go back to your father."

Everything in Mississippi was new for me: the culture, the food, the activities, the students, the Southern accent.

The first time I went through the cafeteria line, I said in

the mixed British accent I had acquired from colonial Hong Kong, "Could I have some po-tah-toes please?"

The girl at the serving line said, "You want some grits?"

To that I replied, "Pardon?"

We stared at each other for what felt like infinity until the girl behind me said, "It's grits! Do you want some grits?" I had no idea what grits were but they looked sort of like mashed potatoes, so I said, "Yes please!" When I sat down at my table and took a mouthful, I paused and looked curiously at the food on my fork. These were not potatoes.

The novelty helped create distance between me and my memories, and soon I narrowed my focus to the future. I decided the college I was in was too small to give me a shot at a good graduate school. So I looked into possibilities for transfers. I was hoping that if I finished in two years I could return home, check on my father for the summer, and then continue with grad school. But what were the odds that I could find another scholarship at a different, larger institution?

Then someone said, "How about Ole Miss? They don't give scholarships to freshmen, but after your first year you're free to apply." I got together my application, they accepted me with a generous offer, and I started preparing to transfer.

My sister Rosita, who also studied at Mississippi University for Women, was upset that I was leaving. For the first time in all of our lives, we would be in different cities. "I'm just going to be a phone call away," I reassured her. But I was worried—my sister tended to find herself in extreme situations involving love and loss. During our first year at college, Rosita had been pursued by a young soldier from a nearby base who asked her to marry him. Though they had only gone out several times, she decided she was in love. They pledged their engagement before he was deployed overseas. He left, and every day she waited for the postman and then ran to the mailbox eagerly to find the letter she knew would be there. But then, suddenly, the letters stopped coming.

She had no idea what had happened to him. Though we lived on different sides of the women's dormitory, my sister began showing up at my dorm room at all hours. She would call me up, tell me she needed me, then ten minutes later she would be slumped on my bed. "Neet, I'm just *sad*," she'd say, over and over again. It comforted me to hear my childhood nickname, but all I could think of was, *Why are we both always so sad? We need to do something so we stop being sad!* Still, we had been trained thoroughly by our upbringing. Rather than go out and blow off steam, we coached each other through our problems. And I lost myself in my homework.

We were good friends to each other that year, and we promised each other that we'd stay in touch once I was at Ole Miss. One weekend, my sister had planned to visit me, but then got stung by a wasp and missed the bus. She called me, sounding disappointed. "Come next weekend," I said. "No big deal. I just have a big test on Saturday, but you can stay with some of my friends off campus on the night I need to study."

As we planned, she came the next weekend, and at two in the morning on Friday I received a call. It was the friend who was hosting my sister. She told me that I needed to come to the apartment right away, saying, "Your sister is totally drunk. She is sitting in the middle of the parking lot and screaming her head off."

I got there as soon as I could. When I arrived, Rosita was sitting cross-legged on the black gravel, shouting, "Mom, where are you? Mom, I'm trying to be strong for Dad and Anita, but Mom, I *can't do it*. Mom! Mom! Somebody, please help me!" My friends didn't know what to do with my frantic sister. I helped them carry her into the house. She sat in a corner of the bathroom and pleaded with them, too drunk to understand that I was there. Falling over onto the tile, she slurred, "Please don't tell Anita. She's studying. Please don't tell her I'm like this." Then she fell asleep on the bathroom floor.

I apologized to my friends, went back to the dorm and was broken hearted over the pain my sister carried secretly as she tried to protect me. I forced myself to block things out that I could not change to focus on getting stronger so I could be more helpful to those needing help. *When I'm the best, I'll be stronger,* I told myself, echoing the words my mother had always said to me. Though I wasn't sure what my life's work would entail, my sister's pain only reminded me of the brokenness in the world and how much work there was to do.

When I arrived at Ole Miss, I had immediately dived into the same routine of disciplined study. I felt alone on the new campus, without the roommate I met in my freshman year staying up until dawn beside me and without the sister I cherished. Although I managed to push myself through, there came a day when I was more than ready to leave Mississippi.

It had all started one weekend in the fall when I had finished all my assignments early and found myself with nothing to do. I wandered alone on campus as the golden leaves fell from the trees. I felt out of place, like I would never be a part of the groups of people who passed me, laughing together and huddling in their coats. This—the ease and carefree entitlement that came so naturally to the college students in my classes—seemed much more difficult to achieve than good grades.

As I walked through a parking lot, I saw a group of students boarding a bus. They looked so friendly that I found myself asking where they were headed.

"We're a church group," one girl said. "Want to come along?"

I made excuses, telling them that I didn't have any money or anything with me, not even a toothbrush. But they insisted that they would take care of anything, and the truth was, I was lonely. As the bus pulled away from campus, I realized I was stuck with them. What was I doing?

It turned out that the weekend was energizing and euphoric. They were a real community, I felt. In their prayers and in their worship I felt traces of the awe and wonder that I'd once felt in the chapel of my mission school. I thought of my mother often that weekend, and began to feel that God had sent me to this group of people to remind me that I was not alone. Like a child, I sought out His presence and found an unknowable, unmistakable joy.

When we got back to campus, my joy faded. *That was just the feeling of having friends again,* I told myself sadly. *It looks like God isn't your answer here.*

Little did I know that God was not a program or a system; rather, He was a person who longed to have a relationship with me—and as with all relationships, it takes time. Forming the relationship means learning about that person and dialoguing with them. I had yet to learn that the only way to develop a relationship with God was to take the time to study the Bible and learn about His character and His purpose. And without understanding that, it was difficult for me to discern God's voice from all the other noise I was hearing.

These early years in the United States gave me new insight into my mother's story. I was rudderless, busy trying to survive; though my brother and his family offered me shelter, I didn't want to impose. So I tried to make it with no family or community to support me and sailed on the power of my own naïveté and hard work. I was still young and trusting, and over and over I found that there were always people who were ready to earn my trust, then shatter it.

The only constant I had from my former life was my uncomplicated, innocent sense of spirituality. I clung to it. I prayed that I would grow stronger in my faith. Yet this was another thing that fell victim to reality. So many times, I found myself desperately trying to reconcile the unpleasant things I saw in the Christian community and the sense of utter peace and power I had felt on those lonely afternoons in the school chapel in Hong Kong.

When I graduated and moved to a new city for one of my first jobs, I was so excited to find a Christian roommate, a girl who seemed completely on fire for God's work. We arranged all the details for our move-in date. She would bring the furniture and would get all the utilities switched on, she told me.

I showed up to the house and waited on the front steps for hours. She never came. I eventually brought my things inside and slept in the dark, on the floor, wondering what was happening.

The next day, I went to a pay phone and called her mother, who picked up and sounded frantic. "Katie broke up with her boyfriend," she said hurriedly. "Well," she went on without waiting for a response. "She wanted to break up with him. She really felt *led* by God to do so. But then she sort of went crazy and thought that she didn't have the strength to live without him and she tried to slit her wrists—it is so awful--so we're in the hospital now. Can I call you back later? Sorry about the apartment."

For a while I was apprehensive about trusting another soul but my loneliness overtook my caution. When a Christian leader I met at a church event asked me out on a date, I decided I could trust him. He was intelligent and composed, and he seemed to have all the answers to any question I asked. I looked up to him.

He was thoughtful, too, and curious about my life story. For the first time, I felt that someone understood what I had gone through to get to America. One day, he came to my apartment and told me that I needed to take a break. "You work too hard," he said, consideration written all over his face. "I have a place where we can go to get away."

When he saw me hesitate, he added, "There's a guest room, don't worry."

The retreat getaway was in the country, a few hours away. We spent all day driving around the green, rolling countryside and talking about ways to solve the world's overwhelming problems. I felt so excited to be in the company of someone with a passion for God and a desire to make a difference. We made dinner together and kept talking, and I went to sleep wondering if I had stumbled upon real love.

I was asleep in the guest room when I was awakened by a hand that was touching me inappropriately. It was pitch-dark, and I cried out sharply, thinking a stranger had entered my room. My friend would come and save me. I yelled his name out and suddenly realized that he was there—that he was the one who was touching me, that his was the voice telling me to be quiet.

I felt completely degraded. I was trembling with panic and adrenaline. I was stuck there with no car and no way to get back to my apartment. I thought immediately of my mother, trapped in her hotel room with the man who raped her. And here I was, trapped with this person I thought of as a friend and a Christian leader.

As my mind raced wildly, he continued to hush me. His hands stayed on my body. I feared for my life. Suddenly I sensed that I was in the presence of one of those fanatics who portrayed one face to the world while hiding a secret disdain for women. For a second my flight instinct took over. Could I run and steal the car and drive away? No—I didn't even know where we were. A thousand thoughts blew through my brain in seconds and I numbed them all.

The next day, he seemed happy and nonchalant, carrying on the same type of personal conversation that we had the day before. I tried to act nonchalant as well, convincing myself that nothing bad really happened. I tried to smile as we ate breakfast, as we got in the car, as he drove me back to my apartment. When we returned, I vowed to never say a word. I knew no one would believe my word over his: the leader was so beloved by all the community.

Instead of raising a protest, I withdrew from the Christian community and raged privately against God. *You feed innocent sheep to the wolves that You appoint to be leaders,* I thought. *You are not fair. You have never been fair.* The memories of that night surged within me when I least expected it, and I would tumble down a rabbit hole of shame and worry and anxiety. A few times, I thought about suicide. *If it was good enough for my mother, it's good enough for me.*

I was on the brink of losing it completely when I got a letter from my father that said he had received positive news from U.S. Immigration on his appeal for residency. Just like that, God's trustworthiness stared me in the face. The dream of coming to America really *would* have been my mother's, had she not acted abruptly to take her own life.

At that moment I saw that I, like her, had forgotten about the long term. I was determined never to repeat her mistake. I was not going to let the act of an imperfect spiritual leader destroy my faith in God. So, I broke off all contact with the man who had hurt me and moved on in my life, believing God to lead me into the future. Humble to the point of passivity, I buried what little dignity I had left.

These incidents made me want to run away from Christians forever. They all seemed like such a well-intentioned but confused group. Where was the power of God in their lives? How could we do good work for God if in the one case we couldn't control our lusts and in the other, we couldn't obey God's voice to break up with a boyfriend without trying to kill ourselves? I began to feel like everyone was just as lost as me; there was no spirituality that could save us all from ourselves.

Through this mental chaos, I could always hear my mother's voice. She used to say, "God is not blind. In the end those who trust Him will win."

But you didn't trust Him, I found myself thinking. *I guess it's up to me to get to the end of your story.*

In those years, my thin thread of trust in God was not enough to support all my good intentions. I failed in many instances where I wanted to be a good example but simply didn't have the strength. Part of the problem was that I almost seemed to be a magnet for the very issues I wanted to get away from, the issues that had haunted me and my family for all my life. Sexual abuse, suicide, hopelessness, violence—they followed me around like faithful, vicious hounds.

In the meantime, my father's life back in Hong Kong was changing rapidly. One day we were talking on the phone about his plans and he informed me that he was thinking of getting remarried. He said, "Loneliness can kill you."

"So, you're really seeing someone, then?" I said quietly, realizing that he was serious. I felt like something was unraveling inside of me, the last thread connecting me to a real family.

He said. "It happened quickly. I was so lonely. I started going to the bar just to talk to people. Then a group of girls at work invited me to go out with them one night, and I met your future step-mother. She's wonderful. She knows my daughters will always be a part of my life. I would never consider this unless I was sure that she will respect your mother and the family we had. We will not have more children." At the point he started saying "will" I knew his remarriage was inevitable.

I don't remember whether or not I was invited to the wedding. Perhaps I was but I didn't have the money for a plane ticket. So the wedding took place without the groom's daughters, and my father started laying plans to send his new wife to America to set up a home for him.

Even back then, I knew that my new step-mother was a peaceful, lovely woman who had unwittingly stepped into an emotionally volatile situation. All she did was fall in love with my father, and suddenly she had decades of family baggage to deal with. More than I could bear to let on, I wrestled with why God allowed the dream of America to go to someone who did not want it as desperately as my mother did.

As much as I needed my father, I did want him to find new happiness. Two years after his marriage, he and my step-mother announced that they were having a baby. At first I was surprised. Hadn't he said I would always be his priority and that he would not have more children? At the same time I realized my father was a new person with his new wife, and I was a remnant from a sadder time. I stopped calling him to talk about my struggles, knowing that he'd just sit on the phone silently and then say, "Okay, I need to go. Bye."

He'd moved on. I hadn't. I felt like a thorn in his side. Why did I have to keep bringing up the past? He had found closure and he wasn't the one to help me find mine.

For many years I wasn't sure how my step-mother fit in my life apart from being married to my father. In hindsight, I was reluctant to get close to her thinking I was betraying my mother. But over time I realized that when my step-mother entered my father's life she was God's gift to my father to fill a loneliness he could not fill with his children.

As for our relationship, I realized that my step-mother never asked questions about my mother and was content not to ask. Her focus was always on walking with her husband and raising the son they had together. Because my father's work required him to be out of the country months at a time, she was left raising her child like a single mother. She did not attempt to blend the families because she was coping with her own adjustments and she saw me as being busy with my own life and adjustments. In this we led independent lives.

Today, we emerge as women entrusted with a mission, not step-mother and step-daughter. We are simply fellow travelers in the journey of life with a mutual love and respect for each other.

After my father remarried, I felt I had lost the only significant male person in my life. I tried to disappear into an intensive new job in a new city. When my youngest brother was born, I saw my father's attention directed to a son and was convinced this was the boy my father always wanted. So, at the age of 23, I escaped into a serious relationship though I was too vulnerable to have one. I was swept off my feet by someone who came into my life like a leading man in a movie. One day, he asked me to lunch; when I returned to my office, there were roses at my desk, with a note that read, "Can't wait to see you again. How about dinner?"

You couldn't wipe the smile off my face all day.

At dinner, and in the months that followed, this man acted like he thought I'd hung the moon. Naturally, I loved it. I bought his flattery and was sailing along in a delightful fantasy world.

Then, out of nowhere, the fairytale crashed to the ground. I was at his townhouse one day when the phone rang and out of pure impulse, I reached to answer it. He immediately grabbed the phone away from me and hung it up.

"Why'd you do that?" I asked.

"Forget it," he said sharply.

It was a sure giveaway. Eventually, I learned that he had multiple girlfriends, one in each city where he traveled for work. He gave me a sob story. "I have a lot of really serious psychological issues," he said, "I have a fear of abandonment. You know, I have this thing with my mother. It helps me to have multiple relationships at the same time. This way, if one leaves, I feel the security of the others. But trust me, you mean the most to me!"

I continued to see him, thinking that we could work this out. I was enraged by his secret life while at the same time I understood the fear of abandonment. But I needed

111

him to choose: break up with the other women or lose me. Shortly after I gave him this choice, he took me home from a date and announced, as I was unbuckling my seatbelt, "I don't want to see you anymore."

This sentence sent my world into a tailspin. He looked at me coldly and said, "Well, I woke up this morning and decided I don't love you anymore." The intensity of the love story dissipated as quickly as it had begun. I stood on the curb as he drove away, and when the tail lights were gone, I was left in darkness.

I realized that I had completely given my heart away. So, how was I supposed to get it back? As much as I wanted to turn the page on this chapter in my life, my new wound was compounded by the unresolved pain of an old wound, a pain that came flooding back as my feelings of abandonment resurfaced. I had never really healed from the death of my mother. I had trusted this man because I desperately needed to trust someone—because I had given my confidences to my mother and now she was dead.

But I'd told him about this tragedy! I thought. *Didn't he care that I did not have the emotional capacity to deal with another betrayal of trust?* I thought about this, then realized that I was foolish to even ask the question. I was just a diversion, and when he no longer found me interesting, my usefulness was gone.

In my apartment, I sat silently on my bed. The darkness wasn't black enough to cover up everything I was feeling. I was so disgusted with myself for needing to be picked by someone, for needing to be special and loved. I'd been passed over by my mother, by my father, and by all these men who weren't interested in a real relationship. My heart beat faster and faster, and I felt myself starting to panic.

I remembered the doctor had given me tranquilizers for my anxiety at work. I decided to take one. I waited five minutes, decided I wasn't feeling any better and took another. *What's wrong with these tranquilizers?* I decided to take five, then ten, then I emptied the entire bottle. All I wanted was for the pain to stop. The next I knew, the room was spinning. My last thought was: *What did I do? Am I going to wake up? Who will even find me?*

The next day, I opened my eyes and couldn't believe that I was alive. I immediately sensed that God had intervened. I got up, got dressed and went to work. The entire day I was filled with awe knowing that God had saved me. But why? Why was I spared?

As I was leaving the office, I pretended to act normally and to have plans for the evening. *How could I have given someone that much power over me?* I was determined to never give myself away like that again. I was responsible for protecting my own heart.

It's funny, but that night finally helped me see both my mother and my father as fellow sojourners. They were never meant to be perfect. They were meant to carry all the hopes and imperfections that come with being human. All the flawed Christians, me included, were the same way, I realized. And although I had on occasion judged my mother for her choices, I now knew better than to ever judge anyone. The greatest tragedies result from a broken heart—and how do you respond to someone with a broken heart? Not with judgment. Instead you pray that God shows mercy, and that they get through it. And you give them all the help you can.

These wilderness years helped me see I needed to deal with my vulnerabilities. I had so much emotional baggage from my mother's suicide, my father's remarriage, and my early betrayals in America. I was in no place to help anyone else or get involved with anyone new; I needed God to heal me first. But these years also gave me a strength I didn't see until much later. My sufferings shaped my calling.

People often ask me how they can figure out what their particular calling is—and I tell them that you can identify your calling in the burdens that God places on you. Sometimes you have to go through the wilderness first. You just have to wait, be patient and allow yourself to be led. We serve best when we let His plan and His mercy pour out through us. The real issue is to get through these wilderness years without removing yourself from the script that God has allowed. God has designed your story to end well, but you can't circumvent the plot line to escape the hard parts. The complication and chaos is there for our refinement, not our destruction.

Most importantly, you cannot jettison the idea that you are the hero or heroine in your own story. With God at your back, you were meant to have a place of significance.

Of course there are moments, or weeks, or even years, when circumstances make this idea hard to grasp. When I stepped onto the soil of America, I felt entirely insignificant. I felt completely displaced. Everything in me wanted to run home. Later, when I felt abandoned and taken advantage of,

I wanted to give up and die. My self-worth was so battered that I couldn't imagine that one day God would redeem all of this heartbreak for something greater. In those days, if you had told me that I would eventually receive a community leader medal from the Daughters of the American Revolution for being an immigrant who changed my new nation—there is no question that I would have laughed sadly.

Little did I know that, when my plane was touching down in New York City and I felt hopelessness crashing in my heart, the conversation in heaven was going entirely differently. God already knew that, decades later, He would open the door for me to establish a ministry to protect the dreams of thousands of women. God knew that all the tragedies I had seen and all the disappointments I would experience were the perfect preparation for the work I would do for Him. While I stared at my situation and assessed it as completely hopeless, heaven celebrated. All the seeds were being planted, and later, all of these seeds would grow.

In this crooked and gloriously fruitful family tree, I can now see that the first seeds were planted long before I was born. My story, and the story of Inspire Women, began on the day my mother, a poor and unwanted village girl, took her first job at the cafe. She was born with the courage and drive to serve others—a trait that, along with all the rest, she passed down to me.

We can't help thinking of the short term, of our own desires. We're human; we focus on the here and now. But God focuses on the life that continues long after our time on earth is over. As I look back, it seems like everyone I met in the wilderness years was taking three steps forward and two steps back. We skip a step, miss a step; sometimes we fall down the steps completely.

Yet through it all, God is there to pick us up and to reconnect the story in ways that will astound us. And so it is with the hundreds of stories the ministry of Inspire Women helps to transform every year. Somehow, someone meets us at a citywide conference, or picks up a book of mine, or hears my message on the radio. Somehow, something catches their attention and they stop in their tracks and take note. They feel drawn to investigate. They discover a place of friendship where someone cares about their unique purpose in life. Someone offers to take the time to help them connect the dots, and map out their future, and envision how they can make the most lasting impact in their community. Someone offers to empower them with additional education they might need, or resources they might need to serve at their highest potential.

And there—just like that—the wilderness ends, and a new life begins.

CHAPTER 6

Dawn after the Darkness

After my near-overdose on tranquilizers in 1979, I gave up on matters of the heart. I was sick of pondering my own weakness. I was tired of thinking that my mother's story was flowing into mine, like a dark and unpredictable river. It was time for a change. Had I not come to this country in search of business success and financial stability? My mother hadn't given up her life so that I could pine over my failed relationships, had she?

So I stopped looking for love. I closed down my vulnerabilities—or so I thought—and ran straight into the cash-filled arms of corporate America. I transferred from my position in Washington D.C. to New Jersey, where I accepted a job at Exxon Corporation.

The year in New Jersey was the easiest that my life had ever felt. The sea was parting for me in the corporate world more than it ever had in real life. My brother, it seemed, had been right about business; it offered a clear path upwards, a clear way to show and achieve success.

Exxon was a good company to work for. My co-workers were smart and enthusiastic and I enjoyed the work I did, designing custom computer applications to solve business problems. My workdays started early and stretched into the night, but I liked the schedule. It kept my mind off things like my family, and the idea of having a personal life.

Then one night, a brutal snowstorm changed all of my plans forever. I was so focused on my latest project that I didn't notice when the snow began falling lightly, then heavily, then in such powerful freezing drifts that the parking lot was an unbroken blanket of white. The few cars that were left were covered completely, and everyone else in the building had left. I had no idea, until suddenly I looked up from my desk to find Bob, a quiet and formal man who worked on the same floor, standing in my doorway with a perplexed expression on his face. I noticed, behind him, that all the lights on our hallway were dimmed. The office was empty.

"What are you doing here? Have you seen how bad this storm is?" Bob asked.

"No," I said, not knowing what else to say to explain why I was oblivious to the storm.

"All the roads are blocked," he said, shaking his head.

"That's fine then!" I said brightly. "I have to finish this report anyway."

He laughed. "You know, this whole building evacuated two hours ago. I don't think you should stay here in the office. I live five minutes away—I can drive slowly in my car. Come on, it's not safe to stay in the office all night."

After I took another look at the snow-covered parking lot, I agreed to leave with him. As we walked down the hall, I racked my brain for everything I'd ever heard about Bob from my coworkers. I knew he had spent a long time working in Europe, and had acquired a formal manner that I found vaguely familiar from my years at the British country club in Hong Kong. He was very tall, and had white-blonde hair and cool green eyes. I realized that there was never any gossip circulating at the office about this man. I knew nothing at all about his personal life. I thought of the awful night I was trapped by the Christian leader in a bedroom and hoped that this night would be nothing like that.

When we got to his townhouse, we shook the snow off our hats and coats and stomped our boots on the doormat and he politely opened the door for me. I was absolutely shocked to find that his place was sparse and immaculate—a far cry from the messy, boyish bachelor apartments that I thought most men my age maintained. Bob walked into the kitchen, calling back, "I'll make us some dinner—are you hungry?"

I told him I would help. His kitchen was just as spotless as the rest of his townhouse, and I marveled further to see that he had meat from a butcher shop and fresh vegetables from the market. We were quiet, not being sure of each other. Then Bob spoke up. "I have a spare bedroom, I should have said that earlier."

"That sounds great," I said. We ate dinner together, speaking only occasionally, both of us surprised, I think, to find ourselves so at ease. That night I locked my door, knowing that I was just being paranoid. But after everything I'd been through, there was no way I was going to take any chances.

The next week, Bob asked me to dinner to discuss a project. He invited me with such polite, businesslike reserve in his voice that I thought there was no chance that it was anything other than a work meeting. When we finished our meal, I reached for my wallet. "You can pay next time," Bob said. I looked at him and saw a surprising glimmer of warmth in his green eyes.

"There's going to be a next time, is there?" I said, smiling, as I put my purse away. In this early swoon of excitement, I felt like I'd stumbled upon some magical secret: a man whose cool eyes turned warm just for me.

In the months that followed, we fell in love, and soon we got engaged. Being around Bob was different than anything I had ever experienced before. He was so kind, so rational, such a good match for me. He didn't shy away from my emotional baggage, but didn't dwell on it either. He was protective without being overbearing. Where other men might have been put off by my tendency to put work above all else in my life, Bob was secure enough to respect my ambitions and kind enough to support me. *My mother would have liked you,* I thought. I wondered if this security was what she had felt with James Jonassen. Slowly, slowly, I felt myself becoming more and more whole.

A few days before our wedding, I called Bob up, feeling nostalgic. "Do you remember that first night we spent together, with the snowstorm?"

He laughed. "You know, I locked my door that night."

"*What?*" I cried, starting to laugh as well. "I locked my door too!"

"I didn't know how liberated of a woman you were," he said sheepishly. "I didn't want to find myself with company in the middle of the night."

"Neither did I," I said, feeling for the thousandth time that I'd found the man I was meant to be with forever.

All of this is to say that you never know what event—a snow storm, a flat tire, a company layoff—has been orchestrated by God to put the right people in your life, or to set you on the path that will eventually result in the mission that He has planned for you. Today, my husband plays a key role in creating the infrastructure of Inspire Women. Without him, the ministry could not be where it is now. I truly believe that God weaves lives together to serve His purpose.

Not long after we got married, Bob got transferred to Belgium. Exxon offered me a position in the Brussels office as well, but I turned it down, shocking everyone in my family and no one so much as Bob.

It was hard to explain my reasoning to people, because my motivations weren't clear even to me. It wasn't that I'd just gotten married and wanted to take some sort of rightful place at home—far from it. It wasn't that I was preparing to have children; it wasn't that I didn't like my job at Exxon. There was just a certain discontent that had persisted no matter how hard I worked at my job. Truly there was no workweek long enough to drown out the feeling I had that something was missing.

Turning down my job came down to this: the closest I had come to feeling content, in my whole life, was in my brief courtship with my husband. I thought that I should pursue this contentment, that I should try to figure out where it was coming from. If achieving financial security hadn't been enough for me, maybe it was time to let all of that go.

We rented a little cottage outside Brussels. I had a little Maltese terrier puppy to keep me company while Bob was at work, and I spent my days going to the market and playing with my dog and tending the sweet, lovely garden that surrounded our new home. It was idyllic, a perfect newlywed life. If only I could have enjoyed it, rather than crying myself to sleep every night!

"What's the matter?" Bob asked me one lazy weekend day, as gently as he could. As usual, I was weeping tears of discontent. I was torn between trying to hide my irrational feelings and knowing that there was no way I could hold this level of frustration inside for long.

"I don't know," I sobbed. "You're perfect. This cottage is so romantic. The neighborhood is so beautiful. I thought that this would be enough."

"But it's not," he said softly.

"No," I cried hopelessly, laughing at myself despite my tears. "It's not even close."

I think a lot of women go through this—knowing that they have aptitude and drive aplenty, but not knowing the right way to use it. I was lost. Was I a wife? Was I a future mother? Was I a career woman? All my life, the dream my mother pounded into me was to reach the free land of America. What was I doing in Belgium? I felt displaced and disconnected from my destiny.

Bob, ever wise and patient, just said, "We'll figure it out."

My dog, in the meantime, was my only consolation. Most of the people in Belgium spoke French and Dutch. I was insecure in the French I had learned at my school in Hong Kong and I spoke no Dutch whatsoever. So, this little pup was the only one I could talk to in my neighborhood. He was peppy and companionable, and sometimes looking at his sweet face was enough to get me to snap out of my black, bleak moods. I took him everywhere: to the post office, to the local stores, up and down the flower-strewn paths for our daily afternoon walk. I even took him with me when Bob and I traveled back to America for the holidays. He was always disoriented for a few days after we got back, walking into walls and shaking his head like there was water in his ears. *My dog gets worse jet lag than I do,* I thought.

One day, shortly after we'd returned from a trip, I let the dog out in the front yard as was my usual practice. However, this time he became disoriented and ran away. All day I ran from house to house, asking if anyone had seen him. I yelled his name until my throat was scratchy and raw. I was trudging up the hill to my house when I saw that the Belgian police were standing at my door. My heart lifted—they'd found him!—until I saw that they weren't carrying my dog at all; rather, they were carrying his collar.

He had been run over on the highway, the policemen said.

That night, I made up my mind. When Bob came home, I met him with a face flushed from tears. "I can't just be here and be your wife," I said. "There's something wrong with me here. It's beautiful but I hate it. I can't speak to anyone. I don't even have a dog anymore. I need to be back in the States, and I need to get back to work."

Was I sure that work was the answer? No, of course I wasn't. In fact, from my previous years in the corporate work force, I knew that work was absolutely *not* the solution to the empty, dark anxiety that kept creeping under all the surface happiness in my life. But at least it kept me busy enough to forget about my heart.

So, I said goodbye to my new husband as soon as Exxon agreed to transfer him back to America at the end of the year. I went back home and lived with his parents for a few months, until I saw an advertisement in the newspaper for a position at Booz Allen and Hamilton, a top management consulting firm. I applied for the job and got it, working all day, all night, all weekend. I was never home; I never had time for anything but work. Even when Bob returned from Belgium, I barely saw him except for the brief, wonderful hours when I'd come home late from work and he'd be waiting for me with dinner on the table. He did this for months and then years, never questioning me, as I worked my anxiety into a manageable level.

Years later, I asked him, "Why did you do all that for me? Why didn't you stop me? Why didn't you say, *Anita, you clearly still have unresolved issues with your mother, and working on Saturdays is never going to change that?*"

He looked at me. "Honey, I just knew that you were looking for who you were. You needed to work, so I wanted to help you. I just wanted to make sure you didn't get sick while you were doing all that."

After three years of working more than 80 hours a week, I was in talks with the management at Booz Allen about a new department they were thinking of starting. They were considering me for the top position, and one day they congratulated me with the news that I'd won this sought-after appointment.

I came home bursting with my news. At the door, my husband greeted me with a huge smile on his face. "I just got a promotion!" he said happily. "But we have to relocate to Houston." I could not believe we were both offered promotions on the same day.

We had some decisions to make and our companies expected an answer the next day.

After all Bob had sacrificed for me, I felt that it was time for me to make a sacrifice for him. I would turn down my big promotion at Booz Allen and start working for Exxon again, this time in Houston.

So, in 1985 we moved to Texas, where the heat was blindingly intense and the skyline was a panorama of industrial prosperity. It was easy to readjust to life at Exxon, and I kept going, fighting through my internal fits of discontentment. I was always looking for something new to take on, something that would fill up the space I felt in my heart. One night I brought up the subject of kids—and to my surprise, Bob told me that he too had been thinking that it was a good time to start trying. Within just a few weeks, I was pregnant.

That summer felt like the hottest summer of all time, and I missed my mother, wondering if this was how she had felt when she was pregnant with me. In September of 1986, I went into labor. We raced to the hospital and I held back tears, thinking that I was a mother now. Would I sacrifice my life for my children like my mother before me? Would I ever disappoint them? Would I ever abandon them?

I prayed for literal deliverance as the doctors put me under, and Bob was the first to see our baby boy. When I woke up, still dazed from labor, I saw our little Robbie—named after my husband—and I thought he looked perfect.

I'd taken nine months of maternity leave from my job. I missed work, but I felt blessed to be able to spend my days with my baby. As the end of my leave approached, I studied every inch of Robbie's little chubby body, memorizing it so that I would always be able to remember him this way. One day he fell over on his play mat, looking just like Humpty Dumpty. "Look at your baby fat!" I cried happily. But then he started making funny noises, struggling to breathe.

I wondered if he had a chest cold, and I took him to the doctor, who immediately sent the nurses rushing around for machines and devices to aid my son's struggles to breathe. "His windpipes are closing," he said. "You need to go to the emergency room right away."

In the hospital, Robbie screamed when the nurses tore him away from me. In the waiting room, I told God that He was cruel for opening my heart to love someone this deeply. I thought about my mother, saying goodbye to her son on the train. Then the doctor came back and told me that Robbie had terrible asthma, and would require skilled supervision for the rest of his infancy and childhood to ensure that his attacks wouldn't be fatal.

And that's when I laid down the deepest need I had, the instinct that I had been trained for all my life. I decided to commit myself to my son and give up my hard-earned financial independence. I knew that this new profession would not come naturally to me. I pictured long hours at home like the lonely days in Belgium, stretching into the future for what seemed like infinity, and it scared me. But I could sense in my heart that my life was changing course. I trusted that I would discover the plan eventually, and I promised my commitment to my son's health in the meantime.

Nineteen months later, my second son Thomas was born. In the confines of my home, surrounded by storyboard projects and timetables for child development, I felt that I could slip into the trap of worshipping my children and turning them into my whole world. I fought to keep the flame of questioning alive, focusing on the longing I felt in my soul. What was I meant to do? What is this potential that I can't put my finger on?

I started wrestling with the idea that there was a divine plan at all. *Either God is real and He has an opinion and a plan for me, and I'm going to honor Him in all my decisions,* I thought, *or He isn't real and I can just forget all this stuff about potential and plans.*

I decided to start studying the Bible as intensely as I had ever studied a case file for Booz Allen. I thought I would give Christianity one full, final effort before deciding whether I was in or out. I wanted to give my children a spiritual structure through which they could organize their world, and I wanted to make sure that all of my knowledge was in the right place.

I thought about one of the Bible verses that I had memorized at the mission school. It was as King David wrote, in the book of Psalm 139:13-16, "For you created my inmost being; you knit me together in my mother's womb. I praise you because I am fearfully and wonderfully made; your works are wonderful, I know that full well. My frame was not hidden from you when I was made in the secret place. When I was woven together in the depths of the earth, your eyes saw my unformed body. All the days ordained for me were written in your book before one of them came to be."

All the days ordained for me—I repeated to myself over and over. I opened the Bible, not knowing that my life was about to change one more time.

In the solitude and reflection that came from studying the Bible, I was able to hear God's voice with startling clarity. And the first thing I realized was that I had been shutting God's true voice out for all of my life—and that had been a great source of my unhappiness. Because of my childhood, I was conditioned to hear only my mother, to let her words resonate like a constant echo in my ears. But I was not born to serve my mother. I was not born to align my life with her goals. No—I was born to serve God.

This was a huge turning point for me. This realization allowed me to acknowledge my wounds and insecurities, to accept them, and to decide to move on with God as my Father instead of as my crutch. Everything started to change when I realized that God's royalty flowed in my veins. *I am the King's daughter first and foremost, and my mother's daughter second,* I told myself, repeating these words so that I would believe them. *My potential lies in one, my flaws in the other—and I live for the King's command.*

The road that opened before me when I began to read the Bible like a family history kept stretching, turning, and pushing me towards new levels of understanding. I became a devoted student of the Bible, then a teacher at weekend Sunday school classes under the tutelage of my wonderful mentor Beth Moore. Wanting to take my education further, I enrolled in seminary, becoming a student again. During seminary, I became involved with a Bible college and began working there while I added to my resume a graduate degree in biblical studies; and as my own kids were getting older. I stayed at the Bible College for five years, finding myself with titles and responsibilities: Director of Women's Ministries, Vice President of Special Programs, Special Assistant to the President. Again, just as I had felt in the corporate world, I was powerfully drawn toward established patterns of progress and leadership. I put faith in the institutions.

The beginnings of Inspire Women were humble and unexpected. One day, a woman who worked in the development office told me, off-hand, that we kept receiving a monthly donation from someone who lived in low-income government housing. She was intrigued by this level of sacrificial giving, and felt sure that there was a story behind it. I did some research and found out that the woman had actually been a student at the college; she'd dropped out of her classes because she could not afford the tuition. She was sending us $25 a month, hoping that her contribution would help someone else stay in school.

I went to ask my director if we could offer this woman a scholarship. "If you raise it through donations, you can offer it," he told me.

I didn't know how to appeal for scholarship funds for an individual. I prayed about it and I felt the Lord impress a certain name on my heart. I called her up out of the blue, and we began talking. "I've been unemployed for eighteen months and I'm inundated with bills," she said.

This was a pretty bad idea, I thought. But God kept pushing me to ask her. I marshaled my courage and said, "I know this may not be a good time, but I just wanted to ask if God might be inviting you to respond to the challenge of a sister in need of a scholarship?"

There was a dead silence. My heart pounded wildly. Then over the phone lines came her response: "I would be happy to do it."

It was a miraculous answer. After that first scholarship, the word got out. God helped me raise the funds to keep multiple students in school, paving the way for a completely unique woman-to-woman network of financial and emotional support.

Then in 2001, the leaders of the college decided that they wanted to hold a citywide women's conference. My immediate thought was that any such thing should certainly reflect the multi-ethnic color of Houston, and although I feared that I lacked the connections to reach every group, I was determined to try.

On the first morning of the conference, the volunteers and I were in place as the sun came up. I was nervous; we all were, never having done anything like this before. One car rolled into the parking lot, then another, then dozens, until the lines were backed out into the road. The women started walking in, striding towards the glass doors of the front entrance like an avalanche descending on us. I still remember the look on the faces of the volunteers. Some of them literally turned white. For one split second, everyone froze and just stared at the scene. And then without a word, everyone went into action and the volunteers did whatever they could to take care of the crowd.

Ultimately, this first Inspire Women's Conference drew nearly 3000 women from over 650 different churches, of which 40% were minorities. Instead of having specific and potentially divisive platforms in the workshops, local leaders of different ethnicities teamed up to co-teach their lessons. Because the leaders united, their audiences united. It was a stunning sight to see.

After two years, as the annual conference gained momentum, the college decided the conference was taking too big a toll on their resources. I was given the option to stay, scrap the conference, and build other programs. Another option was to take the conference with the college's blessing and build it under an independent organization.

I thought of the incredibly diverse group of women who I'd met at each conference—women who needed specific and personal help to be connected to their purpose. Under the umbrella of an independent organization, I could accommodate their unique passions and dreams. I knew I had no choice but to leave. Staying felt safer for me personally but it would kill the progress we had made and future blessings for thousands of God's daughters. I wondered, *Was this how my mother felt when she first thought about leaving China as her only way to protect the family?*

In April of 2003, the college gave me a farewell party and the leaders presented me with an engraved plaque that read: *No single word captures all of who you are. Committed, driven, beautiful, intelligent, articulate, and passionate. But there is one word that will always remind us of you.*

EAGLE. When many are weary, tired and fallen, you will still be flying like an eagle!

In May of 2003, I drove away from the college with all my boxes in my car and tears streaming down my face. I left on a weekend because I couldn't stand to make a fuss. I kept looking in my rearview mirror—the building looked so official, so wonderful. I could almost hear God say, "Are you more impressed with a building than with me?" Honestly, I replied that I was. There was an office in that building, there was a receptionist. *God,* I said, *you're just a spirit!* God must have laughed in heaven. He impressed these words on my heart, "Now you will see what my Spirit can do!"

My biggest battle was my own fear and selfishness. I was scared of charity work, of giving up my life to serve others, especially people who were not even in my biological family! I still had a fierce survival mentality left over from my childhood. Unlike my mother, I didn't have to worry about feeding a family on just a few eggs, but I didn't have the resources to meet the needs of hundreds of people outside of my own family. I was torn between self preservation versus giving my life away to serve others.

I thought about the baby my mother and I once found outside our apartment during a terrible thunderstorm in Hong Kong. The umbilical cord was newly cut. The police said, "It's probably a mother who could not afford to feed the baby and hoping you would take her in." I had begged my mother to keep the baby but was reprimanded for being a dreamer. I saw that my mother was powerless and I definitely felt powerless as a young child. It was years later when the scenes of my childhood years resurfaced and I wondered about that baby's mother. Was she fit to be tied when she saw the police take the baby? Had she hoped she would at least watch her child grow up under our care? What was her story? Did she want to let go of the baby, or was there a man in her life who made her choose? What could she have accomplished with a friend and network to help her make sense of her life after that tragedy? Perhaps because of her once-wounded heart, this woman would be perfectly suited to work with women who have lost children.

Thinking about that night brought me back to another incident I had witnessed as a child, in the alley behind our house. A little girl, only five years old, was put in charge of her toddler brother while her mother worked in the restaurant kitchen. Being barely more than a baby herself, the girl ran off and left him unattended. When she returned, her mother was waiting for her. She tied the small girl's hands behind her back, then roped her feet together. The five-year-old lay on the concrete, which reeked of grime from the kitchen oil. Piles of garbage were scattered on the concrete where she waited, bracing herself against physical punishment.

The kitchen boys were sitting on stools, smoking cigarettes. They were jeering and taking bets on how many times her mother would strike her. Her mother picked up a three-foot bamboo stick, put a toothpick in her mouth, and chewed away as she beat her daughter. "Now will you forget to take care of your brother again?" she shouted.

The little girl screamed her repentance. "No mama!" she blubbered. "Please don't hit me again!" The mother took no notice, and struck the girl again. The girl cried for mercy, but the mother didn't stop.

I was hiding on the balcony of my apartment watching, trembling, just a few years older than her. Then, unexpectedly, the girl turned her head and looked up at the balcony. For a second our eyes met. I will never forget that look in her eyes, glazed and weary and filled with humiliation and shame. I remember running into the apartment begging my mother to intervene. Once again, I was reprimanded and reminded that "There are many problems in the world and we have our own. Mind your own business!" I did not realize then my mother felt defeated and in her helplessness, she chose to look the other way and not overwhelm herself. Meanwhile, God did not spare me witnessing the scene as He was showing me what broke His heart, knowing that one day those tears I had bottled up inside me would find an outlet.

In running Inspire Women, I found myself studying the faces of the women in our audience. From my research on national statistics, I discovered that one out of four women in America has experienced abuse. Though some may hide behind a false front or a hard exterior shell, I saw their pain the way I still remembered the pain in the eyes of that little girl from my yesteryears during a time when her heart was still tender and vulnerable. I think about that child in the alley and I wonder what happened to her. Did she grow up fighting to feel significant? Did she hate her mother? Did she hate her brother? Amongst the women coming to the ministry are there those like her, looking for the love they never received as children? How can I help these women discover a purpose birthed from suffering, so God can transform their past to empower their future?

My mind wandered back to the day I saw Mrs. Tang dragged across the floor as she held on to her husband's ankle. The trauma that beats the dreams out of women is not restricted to any economic level. Even among the rich, I witnessed women who feared to be on their own, who endured adultery and emotional abuse in silence. They tried to look the other way until their hearts could not take it anymore. Would there be women like that who will come to the ministry looking for their true identity and God's purpose for their lives?

During one dark night of self-doubt when I sat with just the idea of a ministry before me, I found myself recalling the story of Dana Curry and Heather Mercer, two women who were taken hostage in Afghanistan. A friend of mine had heard them speak at an event after their release, and called me afterwards to relay their message of hope and purpose. Although time has paraphrased these words, I've never forgotten their essence: "I asked God to send me to do what no one else wanted to do. I asked God to show me what was dear to his heart, and then somehow, I kept hearing the word Afghanistan."

I sensed that God was asking me the same question—asking if I would lay down my own preferences and do what no one else was lining up to do. People often say to me, "I am not called to provide resources for the needy—that's someone else's job!"

In response to statements like this, I always want to shout back, "Would you tell a starving person, 'I'll pray for you!' and let them find their own bread?" It doesn't come easily for anyone to carry the needs of strangers. Yet God, in His mercy, must send someone to risk rejection on the behalf of others who cannot appeal for themselves. We are not always called to do what we like. We don't tell God what job of His we want to apply for. He gets to decide.

As I prayed, I thought about Heather and Dana, meditating on their strength. I thought about my mother, who humbled herself to provide for her siblings. Was she afraid, as a nine-year-old, pleading with her relatives for her family's dinner? Was she afraid when she left Shanghai for Hong Kong with no family and little money for food and lodging? Did she fear for her children's future as she coaxed their way into an acclaimed mission school on the strength of her delicious tea eggs?

Of course she had been afraid, I realized. *True bravery is what happens when you have no guarantees but you keep moving forward.* And at the crossroads of life, I knew I was blessed not just with education resources but with spiritual resources my mother had never had. Where her faith had been based in childish fear and an innate survival instinct— her prayers were like 911 calls—my faith was based on deep knowledge of the Bible and a new understanding of my royal heritage connected to my heavenly Father. My mother, when she felt abandoned and alone, did not have the framework to understand her solitude as a test and that God had a plan to fulfill His purpose.

I knew then that this was exactly the reason I needed to dedicate myself to Inspire Women. God had called me to serve women who, like my mother, needed a friend to walk with them and to help them separate the noise that confused them to discern God's voice for their lives. I wanted so badly for the ministry to ensure that women would never be deceived and lose God's blessings. I wanted them to be sure that our organization would always be in existence so they could count on a friend with the strength to stay.

I thought to myself, *When we feel that everyone close to us has been removed or has chosen to leave—only there can we truly discover what our lives are about. Only there can we truly decide to dedicate ourselves to the work God has planned for us.* I pondered this over and over, realizing that the losses in my life were never meant to destroy me. Instead, they were allowed to prepare me for the birth of something with eternal significance.

It was God who ultimately opened the doors to my life's calling. Inspire Women was established in May of 2003, with zero in the bank, no office space or infrastructure. In the first year, the ministry reached four thousand women. Today, the ministry operates from a permanent headquarters, has reached over thirty-five thousand women, and has funded millions of dollars in scholarships and grants.

In a class I was teaching, I found myself telling the story of Jesus' disciples caught at sea in the middle of a storm. In the midst of the black rain beating down on their faces, they saw someone walking to them on water. At first they were afraid, but Jesus told them not to fear.

Then Peter said these words: "Lord, if it's you, tell me to come to you on the water." Jesus bid him come, and Peter did, starting to walk. He was doing fine until he started looking at the waves. Then he got scared and started to sink. Jesus grabbed his hands and kept him from going under.

"Where Peter went wrong," I said, "was with the word *if*. It should have been *because*. Life takes on a totally new meaning, a different kind of security, when we can say, 'Because it is You, Lord, tell me to come.'"

I too spent forever wondering "if" when I should have been thinking "because." It was always because of God; everything always is. I felt this divine certainty confirmed when I first sensed God wanted me to establish Inspire Women as a perpetual gift in the city of Houston, Texas. But my faith was stretched. I felt God stirring to take the ministry beyond Houston. The very next day, when I was at a business meeting in Dallas seeking the counsel of a company on how to take our ministry global, Heather Mercer walked through the door of the offices. God had brought into my space the physical presence of the very missionary whose life first inspired me to service.

I was shocked into speechlessness.

I felt that God had spoken to me directly through Heather's presence in the office. It was a reminder from God that I had committed to serve Him and now He was giving me the opportunity to do so.

In a subsequent meeting at the same office, the consultant offered up this tidbit about Heather, not realizing her enormous significance to me. He shared what Heather had said to him: how she'd told him that her moment of true freedom came in the jail in Afghanistan. The jails there were unlike jails in the United States. She told him that her cell was dark and terrifying, that she could hear gunshots and people screaming. She knew she couldn't control anything, and this realization made her see the magnitude of God's perspective. Once she accepted that God was in control, she was free.

With that testimony, I embraced God's plan for Inspire Women. Although I did not know the details, I trusted in God's ownership of this story. All I had to do was follow Him.

The fraught and complicated tale of a mother and a daughter and a dream unfolded slowly over the decades of their lives. Both of us were and are deeply imperfect. It wasn't easy to come to grips with the fact that we are fully accountable to God for our own lives. It wasn't easy to untangle the complicated roles that are played in our stories by the people we love. As we strove to be vessels for God's purpose, we struggled to understand where our betrayals and disappointments fit in our dreams.

God doesn't change us instantly. I still bear traces of the scars from my mother's story. Even after I became a dedicated student of the Bible, I had to remind myself every night to trust Him. For a long time, I felt that my life was so complicated. If only I had imagined it through God's eyes as simply a narrative, among billions of others, full of twists and turns and rewards beyond measure. If only I had known that my mother's story, since its painful beginnings long ago, was steadily paving the way for a powerful renewal—not just for me, but for thousands of women across the world.

With this book I put my mother to rest. I put my old self to rest. Sometimes I look around and I wonder why it took me so long. My younger son Thomas once told me, "Mom, you only get sad because you're always thinking about the sad things that happened to you. Just think about the happy things and you'll be fine."

It's not always that simple, is it? The sad things are part of our story as well, and to ignore them is to stay disconnected. We owe it to ourselves to connect the dots, to trust, to rejoice in the lives we were given. And with that, we move to the final chapter: to the other lives of Inspire Women, the individuals who have come to us and found hope in the midst of darkness.

CHAPTER 7

Women, Finding Closure

I grew up under the ever growing shadow of the year 1997...the year that China would reclaim Hong Kong from the British and take it over completely. Fearful of the unknown, my mother dreaded this date, and she reminded me every day that I needed to get the family out of Hong Kong before 1997 came. Of course, you know that it was too late for me to save her and to help her realize her dreams.

As 1997 approached, I thought about her constantly and felt compelled to send for my mother's ashes. I asked a friend who was visiting Hong Kong to bring them back for me, and he agreed. I awaited his arrival with a churning stomach, knowing that I had to come to terms with what remained of my mother and accept that this small, futile gesture was the only way I could get her out.

The doorbell rang. My friend handed me a travel bag and excused himself, saying that he was in a hurry. I shut the door and sat by myself in my living room, in a space washed with sunlight from the windows that stretched from floor to ceiling. Outside the windows was my garden, green and thriving. I was the only one at home.

I unzipped the bag and pulled out a brown padded parcel, heavier than I'd expected. I cut the string, ripped the packet open, and found a white marble urn marked with three letters: R.I.P. I stared at the urn quietly, then closed my eyes, feeling the golden light from the day on my face, on my arms.

To my utter surprise, the old emotions didn't come flooding out. I actually did feel peace. I realized that God had done His work in my life. I had grown into a woman who could cope, who could deal with the bleakest situation head-on with courage and without judgment.

This peace is what God has been offering me all along, I thought. *This peace is the end of my mother's story, the result of her final, tragic choice being transformed into the passion that helps me drive this ministry.* I thought about the women I now call friends, the women who had been affirmed and empowered, life after life after life.

The individuals drawn to Inspire Women come from every possible background you could imagine. Across racial, ethnic, economic, and national identities, they choose to be part of an organization where none of that matters. These women may have little in common from their pasts, but their futures are united under a common goal: to make something more out of their life, to live up to their potential, to trust in the common bond of the royal lineage that comes from being a child of God. They feel the urgent call to turn their past obstacles into new promise, renewal, and hope. They are all part of creating this unique community, where the superficial is truly cast aside and the souls of women can be unburdened.

To the men reading this book, think about your wife, your sister, your mother, or your daughter. Do you know a woman who is bursting with potential, who just needs someone to affirm her, and encourage her to step out in faith?

To the women reading this book: are you yourself ready to move forward unhindered into your future? Do you need support in putting old issues to rest so that you can find your story? Do you have a daughter, a niece, a neighbor, a best friend, a pastor's wife, or a coworker who needs to be encouraged to discover and to live God's purpose?

Below are just two stories out of thousands, voices shouting with joy and courage to proclaim that women are God's children, daughters of a King, destined from birth to change the world. (Some facts in these testimonials have been combined or altered, in order to protect the identity of the individuals.)

I often think of the story of one woman I'll call Jenny: a petite blonde executive with a shy smile and an unshakable air of confidence. Beneath her veneer of wealth and security is a tangle of painful family memories.

One of her earliest memories, she told me, was a car coming for her mother and taking her away to a mental hospital. She remembers standing small in her doorway with her father, watching her mother look back at the two of them from the car window. Just a young child, she felt panic and a deep loneliness set in as the car drove down the road and disappeared around a leafy corner.

For the next few years, Jenny's mother stayed away, locked in the institution. Her father went to visit, but Jenny wasn't allowed. Growing up in her suburban neighborhood in the Midwest, Jenny tried her best to carry out the normal activities of a normal kid, all the while wondering what was wrong with her mother, and why it was taking so long to fix.

But then Jenny's mother came home. Jenny's initial giddiness and joy was quickly overridden by the responsibility of making sure that home was always an artificially pleasant environment. Her father told her that any argument or problem could set off her mother's mental illness, and the best thing for the family would be a calm house, where no one complained or raised their voice.

Entrusted with the responsibility of keeping her mother from another mental breakdown, Jenny became the perfect kid, suppressing her problems and only talking about positive things. She hadn't even turned ten yet and there were times when she felt scared and irrational and simply bratty, but she always just looked at her mother's face and reminded herself that she wasn't allowed to have issues.

When Jenny was eleven, her father asked her if she'd go on a little trip with him. He needed a quick favor. "Your mother and I haven't been able to do certain things with each other for a long time," he said.

He took her to his office on a weekend and instructed her to remove her clothes. She obeyed out of fear. As he started to touch her, she shut her eyes and willed the encounter to end. When it was over, she held in her tears for the long car ride home as her father turned up the radio, singing along to oldies with a lightness and joy in his voice. She held her tears as she walked into the house with him, kissed her mother, who was vacantly knitting at the windowsill. She kept it together until she was able to retreat to her bedroom, where eleven-year-old Jenny cried for hours in the throes of a nameless shame. Maybe her father had gone crazy too. That's what had happened. But he wasn't the crazy one, and it would never happen again.

Of course, though, it did. It went on for months. She thought about telling her mother, but her determination to keep the house peaceful was too strong. Instead, Jenny started creating an elaborate getaway plan. She wrote letters to her aunt, who had recently gotten married in a different city. She stole money from both of her parents until she had enough to feel safe, and one day, she simply ran away. She got on a bus with her aunt's address on a slip of paper in her pocket and a big duffel bag at her feet. As the bus pulled away from the station and rolled into the country, Jenny was afraid, but mostly she was excited. Finally she would be safe.

At this time she was still just eleven—motherless, rudderless, and already a hardened expert at survival.

When she arrived at her aunt's house, she was greeted with open arms. Her aunt was young and pretty, a sales agent for a local insurance company. Her aunt's husband was handsome and polite. The two of them had just adopted

145

a fat border collie who nuzzled up to Jenny, licking her hand. It was like paradise. Jenny went to sleep that night in their guest room feeling peaceful and happy, dozing off as her sighs of relief grew synchronized with the dog's breathing.

The next morning, Jenny had breakfast with the couple and then went back to her room to think, saying goodbye to her aunt, who was driving off to work. She went through all the stuff in her bag, counting her money and thinking about what her next move should be. She imagined asking her aunt to adopt her, starting a new school where she would come in as the confident, smiling new girl and make lots of friends.

Suddenly the bedroom door opened and her aunt's husband came in. "So, you think you're just going to live here without paying for it?" he asked.

Jenny felt her world collapsing around her, as the man pushed her onto the bed. She had vowed that this would never happen to her again. She fought him, bit him, screamed and cried out. But there was nothing she could do—he was too strong. He told her to just relax and stop fighting it. She cried and cried and cried and cried as he continued to rape her.

"If you tell my wife, I'll kill you in your sleep," he said casually, zipping up his pants and leaving.

By this point, Jenny already wanted to die.

Jenny had escaped a burning building only to run straight into another one. She was raped repeatedly in her aunt's house for one impossible week until she was able to contact a friend, who gave her a true safe haven.

Today, Jenny is a high-level executive. She has forgiven her father, after he came to her and begged her pardon for what he now sees as a period of brief and terrible insanity.

She let go of her hate for her aunt's husband after hearing about his breakdown: a few years after he violated her, he got into his truck, locked the doors, took out a gun and shot himself. When she received a phone call telling her about his death, she saw he had turned his violence against himself, and was able to feel sorrow rather than satisfaction.

She moved on in her own life. Then she came to an Inspire Women event where I was giving a message on being free from regrets of what could have been or fears of what could happen. "So many times," I said, "we think if only, if only. If only I didn't come from a dysfunctional family, if only I had gotten the job I wanted, if only someone hadn't abused me, if only...Or we live in the world of our imaginary fears and we are crippled by 'What if's'. What if I can't save my mom? What if I fail? What if I get sick? But, what if we started thinking 'Even if'? Even if I was hurt terribly, my life is far from over, and my potential is in no way spent. Even if the world crumbles around me, I will stand because God will get me through it."

Jenny got involved with the organization that day. Through Inspire Women, she has made sense of her suffering. She sees her past as giving her insight and compassion for other women who are struggling to get past childhood wounds. Over and over, she has served as the benefactor for other formerly abused women who desired to be trained to return to their past to rescue women living in circumstances they have overcome. She has spent her life both achieving and serving, letting go of her bitterness without erasing her suffering. How beautiful is that?

✺

I recall vividly the face of a woman named Faith. When her mother died her father abandoned her and two siblings for several months. She was a young child herself who was filled with panic over the care of her seven year old brother and five year old sister. She was eleven at the time. She said, "I didn't know what to do. We held each other in the apartment and sat there in the dark because the electricity had been turned off. We didn't have any money to buy food. So I went knocking on the doors of the neighbors offering to do chores in exchange for food."

Only the grace of God could have carried a young child through such an ordeal. And that same grace protected her and her siblings through three months of hell until her father returned for the family. She walked into my office a woman in her thirties carrying a secret with deep emotional scars that were invisible to the world. She was crying out for an identity grounded in God's word to erase the feelings of unworthiness ingrained in her from her formative years. Under all the pain, her soul felt a stirring that the world was bigger than her pain. She was like a bird with a broken wing who suspected she was really an eagle and if someone could help her believe in God's plans for her, she could believe them as well. She asked for a scholarship to be trained to work with abused kids. From her past suffering, she found her purpose.

✺

Hundreds of stories like these flow out of every Inspire Women gathering, which occur year-round, on scales both enormous and small. These women are living proof of how rare and transformative it is to find an organization where you feel you belong, where somehow your soul is set free to soar when you begin in a place of unconditional love and acceptance.

Someone once asked me to sum up my ministry in a few sentences, and to my surprise the words came easily.

"Imagine a world the way God intended where any woman regardless of ethnicity or economic level is empowered to soar at her potential without artificial barriers imposed on her and where she has a friend to walk with her and invest in her to change the world," I said, realizing that this was the dream that had been set in motion for me the day my mother died. "I commit to building an organization that will accomplish these goals. I will continue to work to make Inspire Women a perpetual gift for generations to come."

The vision of awakening God's purpose in women across the world is daunting. This dream is bigger than any I have ever had before. What gives me the courage is to know that God works through relationships and He puts the right people around me so we can take the hill together. I find comfort in knowing God has already gone before us. He is the Master planner. He is the one responsible for results and we get to offer Him our obedience.

The Bible tells me in the book of Ephesians chapter 2, verse 10 that we were created to do good works. However, our good works do not result from our striving or efforts to win God's approval. It results from being in God's presence like the way I used to look into my mother's eyes and saw what her heart longed for and simply wanted to give her the dream she so desired. I pray that my service will be fueled by the heart of a daughter who is simply saying, "Father, send me!"

Epilogue

Shortly after my mother died, I found a tin biscuit box hidden at the back of our refrigerator. In it were pieces of jewelry that she had hoarded over the years as an emergency fund, to be sold in times of need. Underneath the gold pieces was a note, addressed to her children.

It was simple—written, no doubt, in the confused and desperate last days of her life. *This is for my children Bobby, Anita and Rosita, for their future in the United States.* My heart clenched when I read those words, trying to decipher if there was any significance in the order of our names. I dwelled on them for decades. I saw the treasure box as the only thing my mother had left me.

But then, one day, as I was wrestling with my own life, I walked suddenly into a moment of clarity. My mother's story was its own hidden treasure. She must have known that one day, I would find it, just as I found that box.

I began to piece her life back together and in the process, to reassemble my own. As I brought her back in my memories, I could almost touch her, see her, and smell the perfume she used to wear. I walked with her through her girlhood in the village, through the brief beautiful dreams that were fulfilled and the many more that were lost forever. From the ashes of the stories she had told only me after the rest of the family had gone to sleep, emerged a story of love and trauma and betrayal and disappointment—a story that can finally be put to rest by her daughter's attempt to write the ending.

The ending is unfolding before us, in my mother's grand-children, in the foundation of a ministry that will protect God's dreams for thousands of women, beginning in Houston, Texas and spreading to cities across the nation and the world. The realization hit me like a thunderbolt: that my mother's life, for all its losses, had never once lost its central, extraordinary idea. In this world of tragedy, the best we can do is look out for each other; the highest act of friendship we can perform is to help those we love.

I no longer blame my mother for her final act of self-destruction. Rather, I choose to love her for all the pain she endured until it became unbearable. I find hope in the fact that God did remember her prayers to protect her children. Her son, abandoned to unwilling relatives while she was fighting for survival in Hong Kong, made it to America with nothing, and worked his way up to a senior executive position at a fortune 500 company. Her older daughter began in nursing, then left her profession to raise her two children. She finds joy in play-ing tennis and working in a tennis club. And my mother's spirit and ashes are finally united with her children in America.

And then there is me, her youngest daughter, the one she trusted with her secrets. I carry with me her service and leave behind her limitations. All of her dreams came true for me. I have the opportunities, the education, and the loving and sup-portive family that she always wanted for me.

In understanding the purpose of my mother's life I under-stood better the purpose of mine. Her life unfolded in front of me like a screen play which represented the lives of millions of women. She was powerless in a culture that shamed her and rejected as polluted for being a victim. She believed the lies of the world when God wanted her to believe Him. But she had no chance to truly know Him because she didn't read His love letters to her. Some mothers' lives were meant to leave a legacy for us to continue; others suffered so their children would choose differently. My mother suffered to pave the way for a different life for me. She begged for rice for her siblings so they wouldn't have to. She was willing to take the risk to ensure a better life for the rest of the family. Her mistake was she gave up too soon and lost the blessing God intended for her. But in spite of one fatal wrong choice, she taught me selfless service. She taught me to have the courage to take a chance to build a better life. And through this lasting gift to me, she planted the seeds for a transcendent God-given passion to help women find a reason to live and a reason to die that is connected with our creator.

Although mine is a mother-daughter story, I hope this book will encourage you to connect the dangling threads of any broken story in your life and find closure. I hope it will serve as a catalyst for conversations between mothers and daughters for healing and greater understanding. I hope it will bring about an old forgiveness, allowing us to understand and recognize our mothers as women who had struggles of their own. Most importantly, I hope this book provides those who read it the strength to look at their own story and accept the extraordinary potential that lies in the part of it yet to come.

As I lay my mother's story to rest, I accept the journey God has given me. I trust His guidance to help me make the next right choice, one choice at a time. I pray that I will finish this story well.

Friend, I pray the same for you!

Sample Discussion Questions

CHAPTER 1: **Born a Daughter**

Below are sample questions for chapter 1. If you find these questions helpful and would like discussion questions for the remaining chapters of this book, please visit www.inspirewomen.org or call 713-521-1609.

1. Have you ever found life unfair because you feel things should be different or that you should not be in the situation you are in? What action can you take to respond to the current challenges in life as you assess them to be today and stop wasting emotional energy agonizing over what life should be?

2. Who in the family usually rises up to save the day? What does the scripture from Luke 12:48 "From everyone who has been given much, much will be demanded; and from the one who has been entrusted with much, much more will be asked." mean to you? How do you define enabling versus using what God has given you to express mercy?

3. What fears or insecurities do you see in yourself that were in your mother or a significant person in your life? Are your fears warranted based on your life and current situation? Or are you living in someone else's world and detached from your own?

4. Are you excited to be born in this time and age? If so, why? If not, why not? What do you see as empowering or limiting because of the time in history in which you were born? What must you change to align your self-image with how God views you?

About Anita Carman

Anita and her family when her sons were in high school. Photo by Alvin Gee Photography.

From the founder and President of Inspire Women, a nonprofit that transforms thousands of lives, comes this heart rending, keenly honest, and ultimately hopeful story of a mother who dared to dream through unimaginable struggles. In a novelized approach to tell a powerful story, Anita Carman leads readers to explore what it means to define a life, a purpose, and a passion.

Anita is married with two grown sons. She earned a Masters of Business Administration from the State University of New York and pursued a life of corporate success at major companies including ExxonMobil and Booz Allen &

Hamilton. She left her corporate career to raise her children, heal from her mother's tragic suicide, and search for God's ultimate purpose for her own life. In preparation for a call to full-time ministry, Anita earned a graduate degree from Dallas Theological Seminary where she graduated at the top of her class.

In May of 2003, Anita founded Inspire Women with no money in the bank, but a crystal-clear mission to inspire women of all ethnicities, denominations, and economic levels to find and pursue their God-given purpose.

With a special focus on mentorship and funding, each year Inspire Women disciples hundreds of leaders and funds scholarships and grants for a singular purpose, to invest in women who change the world. Inspire Women has a heart for women and devotes its time and resources to helping them realize their God-given potential.

In 2007, Anita was awarded a community leader medal from the Daughters of the American Revolution for being an immigrant who changed America.

Anita says, "God breathed eternity into us. We were made for big dreams with eternal consequences. If you want to rise above the pain in your own story, let God make your story bigger! May your pain serve as your catalyst to change the world!" Anita is also author of *Transforming for a Purpose: Fulfilling God's Mission as Daughters of the King*, published by Moody Publishers.

157

About Inspire Women

Inspire Women is a 501(c)3 organization that exists to awaken God's purpose in women of all ethnicities, denominations, and economic levels to help them live out their purpose and change the world.

We inspire women to find their spark in a multi-ethnic multi-denominational conference that reflects an environment where women are empowered to soar at their potential with no artificial barriers, impacting the world as God intended.

We fund potential by investing in women through scholarships for leadership training and tuition for seminary.

We fuel God's mission with regular gatherings to keep leaders serving, and to support new leaders through ministry grants.

To hear a daily word of inspiration from Anita Carman, please download the free Inspire Women app.
For a free copy of Anita Carman's conference keynote message *Beyond My Mother's Dream* and/or to sign up for Anita's weekly e-devotional, email **Anita@inspirewomen.org** or call **713-521-1609**.
For other books written by Anita, please visit **www.inspirewomen.org**.

Inspire Women's Leadership Academy

**Has God entrusted you with a dream?
Do you need to overcome emotions that could
derail you from your mission?**

At **Inspire Women's Leadership Academy** you will learn:

- To operate out of your identity as daughter of the King

- To follow proven steps to process your pain of loneliness, rejection or fear

- To fortify your heart as keeper of the vision

- To respond to life according God's family code of behavior

- To develop the emotional fortitude to finish well

For more information on
Inspire Women's one-year Leadership Certificate
(on site in Houston, Texas or online via distance learning),
please call 713-521-1609 or visit **www.inspirewomen.org**.

Personal Notes

Made in the USA
San Bernardino, CA
24 January 2017